psalms

A **SIMPLY BIBLE** STUDY

CARMEN BEASLEY

To Jesus Christ our Lord,

He lifted me out of the slimy pit,
out of the mud and mire;
he set my feet on a rock
and gave me a firm place to stand.
He put a new song in my mouth,
a hymn of praise to our God.
Many will see and fear the LORD
and put their trust in him.

PSALM 40:2-3 NIV

And to my Mom and all our loved ones who have gone before us, to sing new songs in His presence.

Blessed is the one
who trusts in the LORD

PSALM 40:4 NIV

SING TO THE LORD A

NEW SONG;

SING TO THE LORD,

ALL THE EARTH.

PSALM 96:1

table of *contents*

PSALMS | A **SIMPLY BIBLE** STUDY

INTRODUCTION

STUDY CONTENT

APPENDIX

OH, FEAR THE LORD,
YOU HIS SAINTS, FOR
THOSE WHO FEAR HIM
HAVE NO LACK!

PSALM 34:9

welcome

LEARNING A NEW SONG

welcome to *psalms*

LEARNING A NEW SONG

Dear friend, thank you for joining this journey TO KNOW GOD through the Psalms. This Bible study is about God's song. It's about the hymns and prayers of the psalmist that carry us heavenward and lift our eyes towards Jesus, the One who authors and perfects our faith.

Whether struggling in pain and sorrow or dancing with gladness and joy, whether confused and angry or overflowing in peace and love, the psalmist sings. Wholeheartedly, the psalmist pours out praise. And just as wholeheartedly, he pours out his lament. He cries, weeps, mourns, and vents his anger, sorrow, or shame until reaching a point of complete surrender and trust in God.

Indeed, a psalm reflects the heart transformation of the psalmist. He walks through a process of mourning until moved to trust God with confidence. In the end, the psalmist's song and heart become intermingled with praise towards God.

As 21st-century believers, most of us have not learned the skill of praying to God until reaching the point of surrender. To admit our need, expose our naked hearts, and bare our souls is humbling. No different from Adam and Eve seeking to cover up their hot-mess state, we prefer to hide. Who doesn't prefer the happy songs, songs of joy and victory?

Yet skipping the pain and jumping straight to joy often masks reality, and it can be pretentious. Similar to Adam and Eve's covering of fig leaves, the result is futile. We don't arrive at the songs of joy and victory without first walking through pain and suffering. In fact, the song of joy is meaningless without first being honest and identifying the sorrow and suffering that preceeds it. The psalmist understood this.

Walking is key. Rather than remaining stuck in grief or pain or shame, day after day singing the same dreary dirge, the psalmist moves through the pain. Friend, with God's gentle grace and illuminous truth, may we learn to do the same. May we learn to sing the Lord a new song.

Personally, I became more aware of God's song while losing my mom to cancer. One life incomprehensibly touches countless other lives. The classic movie *It's a Wonderful Life* depicts that profound idea as George Bailey's family and friends rally around him during a low point in his life's journey. Like George, Mom's life touched the lives of many in both small and big ways. The bigger ways involved being a wife, a daughter, a sister, a mom, and a "nana." For some of us, our lives have never been, nor will they be, the same. We continue to miss her presence.

Throughout the years, I have longed to share my joys and sorrows and discuss countless experiences with Mom. Perhaps these things won't be important to discuss in heaven, where we will all sing new songs of a different kind, but the longing is real. I imagine heaven as not only being present with the Lord, but being present with all of God's children, including Mom and our other loved ones who have gone before us.

Paul tells us that our dear ones who believed in Jesus Christ as Lord, upon leaving their bodies and our presence here on earth, are immediately ushered into the Lord's presence and at home with him (II Corinthians 5:8). Mom clung to that hope:

> Therefore, we do not lose heart. Though outwardly we are wasting away, yet inwardly we are being renewed day by day. For our light and momentary troubles are achieving for us an eternal glory that far outweighs them all. So we fix our eyes not on what is seen, but on what is unseen, since what is seen is temporary, but what is unseen is eternal.
>
> II CORINTHIANS 4:16-18 NIV

In the midst of helping Dad care for Mom in her final months, many friends rallied and blessed us with their prayers, words of encouragement, and acts of kindness. What a gift! Many of you have experienced similar circumstances and understand. These dear friends helped to anchor us in the Lord.

One particular note from those days resonated with my heart, and I have never forgotten it. This special friend wrote, "I'm praying each day that the Lord gives you His song in your heart." In answer to her prayer, God graciously provided. The songs came. My heart responded with songs of honest grief and tears. Other times, my heart offered songs of praise and thanks to a God who was faithful in the midst of sickness and death. These songs became prayers of worship. Prayers of confidence. Prayers of eternal hope.

Psalm 42:8 became a reality in my heart:

> By day the Lord commands his steadfast love, and at night his song is with me, a prayer to the God of my life.
>
> PSALM 42:8

To this day, I pray this same prayer over the lives of loved ones. Dear reader, I am also praying this same prayer for you.

MAY GOD GRANT US HIS SONG IN OUR HEARTS.

Songs, whether secular or spiritual, reflect life's experiences and our feelings as we journey through these experiences. During the quarantine of the COVID-19 virus, a YouTube video humorously circulated of a four-year old boy fixing himself a sandwich while singing "All by Myself." The chorus croons like this:

All by myself | Don't wanna be | All by myself | Anymore

Eric Carmen originally sung this song. Released in 1975, it skyrocketed in popularity as I was trekking my way through junior high school. And so, the video of this little boy caught my attention. I had forgotten this song. I chuckled as I remembered being a young teen, with the tumultuous feelings that often accompany the territory of that age. Oh! How I melodramatically listened to and identified with the sad lyrics while feeling very alone in my bedroom with schoolwork. Now this pintsized, four-year old boy, tired of being quarantined and separated from his friends, zeroed in on the singer's emotions and words. During the pandemic, the light-hearted video brought cheer to many in the midst of uncertain days, and quite frankly, very real suffering and isolation.

Isn't it amazing how hearing an old tune can take us back in time like that? Particular songs bring fond memories of dating my husband. Other songs highlight seasons of growth in my relationship with Jesus. How do songs tap into our feelings so? Elena Mannes, author of *The Power of Music*, says that scientists have found that music stimulates more parts of the brain than any other human activity. [1]

Melodies are important, but so are the lyrics. Whether experiencing joy, sadness, anger, fear, trust, distrust, surprise, or anticipation, the poetry of music ignites and resonates with the wide gamut of our emotions. Finally, tying it altogether, song typically involves rhythm and cadence, which seem to drill and fasten both the melodies and lyrics into our brains. Have you ever had a song stuck in your head? Then you understand! Rarely does the same phenomenon happen with mere spoken text.

Song is powerfully communal, too. In his book *Music and the Mind*, Anthony Storr stresses that a primary function of music is collective and communal, to bring and bind people together. Rock concerts effectively display this binding, connective power, where thousands of people are moved in solidarity to the excitement of the music. [2]

---

[1] https://www.npr.org/2011/06/01/136859090/the-power-of-music-to-affect-the-brain
[2] https://academic.oup.com/brain/article/129/10/2528/292982

THE PSALMS ARE NO DIFFERENT.

If God wanted to knit His people's hearts and minds together with His and with one another, what means do you suppose He might choose? Song sounds downright perfect, doesn't it?

The Psalms, a collection of prayers found in the middle of our Bibles, belong to the biblical genre of wisdom literature written in Hebrew poetry. Back in their heyday, the psalms were set to music. Using rhythm, cadence, lyrics, and melodies, God provided these songs; songs intended to be "stuck" in both heads and hearts as a liturgical means of both individual and communal worship. Although the musical aspect of these songs is lost today, the book of Psalms continues to connect and bind generations of God's people in unity with God and one another.

The psalms are gut-wrenchingly honest. Nothing appears cleaned-up. Sin is never "swept under the rug." Like the rest of the Bible, the raw edges of man and the messiness of his fallen state remain exposed for all the world to see.

In his book *How to Pray: A Simple Guide for Normal People*, Pete Greig says, "The Bible is often more honest than the church. Many of the Psalms are not happy-clappy songs but cries of unresolved pain." Rather than allowing the emotions of life to become pent-up inside, these songs help God's people learn to seek His presence and work through trials.

Honesty with God, with others, and even with ourselves is not easily attained. Yet, the psalmists intuitively mastered vulnerability by praying what Dr. Larry Crabb deems "papa prayers," the prayers to our Heavenly Father that forgo pretension, purge anything hindering our relationship with Him, and see God as our most valuable treasure. [1]

---

[1] Crabb, Larry. (2006) *The Papa Prayer: The Prayer You've Never Prayed*. Nashville, TN: Thomas Nelson Publisher, p.10.

Throughout the book of Psalms, the Hebrew people honestly express to God, every human emotion possible. There is no holding back! Whether shamelessly expressing pain or boldly proclaiming joy, the songs of the psalmist teach us how to do the same.

THE PSALMS ARE WORTHY OF OUR STUDY.

In *Prayerbook of the Bible*, Dietrich Bonhoeffer highlights the teaching aspect of the Psalms: "The richness of the Word of God ought to determine our prayer, not the poverty of our heart." He notes how astonishing it is that a prayer book is included in the Bible: "This is pure grace, that God tells us how we can speak with him and have fellowship with him." He points to Martin Luther who held to the following position:

> But whoever has begun to pray the Psalter earnestly
> and regularly will "soon take leave" of those other
> light and personal little devotional prayers and say:
> Ah, there is not the juice, the strength, the passion,
> the fire which I find in the Psalter. Anything else
> tastes too cold and too hard.
>
> MARTIN LUTHER [1]

Oftentimes, the Psalms can be found bound together as one book with the New Testament. This is understandable. Jesus Christ Himself told us that the Psalms point to him (Luke 24:44). And He Himself prayed and sang these very songs to His dear Father. Even while hanging on the cross, our Savior died with words from the Psalms on his lips (Psalm 31:5, Luke 23:46). [2]

[1,2]   Bonhoeffer, D. (1996). *Life Together and Prayerbook of the Bible.* (G. L. Müller, A. Schönherr, & G. B. Kelly, Eds., D. W. Bloesch & J. H. Burtness, Trans.) (Vol. 5, p. 161). Minneapolis, MN: Fortress Press.

ARE YOU IN NEED OF A NEW SONG?

Then welcome to the Psalms! Whether in the midst of a dry and weary land or overflowing with joy and thanksgiving, these prayers can be used to draw near to God and connect with generations of God's people.

When we pray a psalm, not only do we pray with David, but we pray with Jesus Christ Himself. We also pray with generations of our brothers and sisters in Christ. These songs bind and connect our hearts as one.

I have loved pouring through the Psalms. And yet, it is with great trepidation that I offer this book. Dietrich Bonhoeffer cautions:

> Where we no longer pray the Psalms in our churches, we must take the Psalter that much more into our daily morning and evening worship. Every day we should read and pray several psalms, if possible with others, so that we read through this book repeatedly during the year and continue to delve into it ever more deeply. We also ought not to select psalms at our own discretion, exhibiting disrespect to the prayerbook of the Bible and thinking that we know better than even God does what we should pray.
>
> DIETRICH BONHOEFFER [1]

---

[1]   Bonhoeffer, D. (1996). *Life Together and Prayerbook of the Bible.* (G. L. Müller, A. Schönherr, & G. B. Kelly, Eds., D. W. Bloesch & J. H. Burtness, Trans.) (Vol. 5, p. 161). Minneapolis, MN: Fortress Press.

And so, my trepidation comes from the need to pare and organize various selections of the psalms for the purpose of Bible study. Rather than reviewing all 150 psalms, this book is organized by categories of psalms. After completing this study, you will be well equipped to follow Bonhoeffer's advice in regularly praying through the psalms.

This book is arranged like other SIMPLY BIBLE books. Please use the next part of the introduction to become familiar with the inductive Bible study process. If you are already familiar with this study technique, a humble review often proves helpful. Sometimes familiarity can breed contempt. Please don't let that happen with Bible study! Even after several years of teaching inductive study, I still feel like I have so much more to learn.

So read through the steps of inductive study. Then be sure to read the section titled *Putting Psalms in Context*. This study addresses a new biblical genre for SIMPLY BIBLE: the genre of poetry. *Putting Psalms in Context* will delve into the particulars of Hebrew poetry and is critical for preparing you to get the most out of this study.

As we begin, let's remember that even though this is called a Bible "study," we are seeking more than just knowledge about God and His Word. We are seeking a relationship with Him. In a similar way that I have longed to share my joys and sorrows and discuss countless experiences with Mom, I can do that today with God. He is present. Just as my mom enjoyed sharing thoughts, hearts, and time together, so does our Good Shepherd. Friends, let us draw near to Him that He may put His new song in our hearts!

Again, welcome. I am excited to fully embrace the hope of Jesus Christ with you. Prayerfully and with joyful anticipation,

Carmen

PS—For more Bible study tips, please visit our online community at **Facebook: Simply Bible Study Group, YouTube: Simply Bible Channel,** or **simplybiblestudy.com.**

LORD, MAY DAVID'S CRY BE OUR CRY! May we long for You as we prepare to study the Psalms. Lord, incline Your ear to us as we seek You. Through this study, help us learn to seek You with all of our heart, soul, mind, and strength. May we learn to be real with You and real with ourselves. Draw us out of whatever miry bogs we are in, especially those of inward thoughts and self-destruction. Lord, lift our eyes to see You. Set our feet upon the rock of Your salvation. Lead us and make our steps secure. Lord, put Your new song in our mouths, a song of praise to You, our Almighty God. Transform us and make us new, such that You will be glorified and many will see and fear and put their trust in You.

before we *begin*

Add your perspective to this prayer. How do you hope to be transformed—to *think* and *live* differently—because of this study?

....

....

....

....

inductive study

AN INTRODUCTION TO **SIMPLY BIBLE**

SOME TRUST IN CHARIOTS
AND SOME IN HORSES,
BUT WE TRUST IN THE NAME
OF THE LORD OUR GOD.

PSALM 20:7

inductive bible study

AN INTRODUCTION TO **SIMPLY BIBLE**

AS A LITTLE GIRL, I ADORED COLORING BOOKS. Smooth, crisp white pages displayed bold black lines of perfectly-drawn figures and characters. The spaces patiently awaited color. Fondly, I remember the joy of opening a new pack of crayons. The waxy smell and the neat little rows of pointed tips colorfully peeked out and tantalized me as if to say, "Try to choose just one!" Creativity awaited. Or so I thought.

When my four children were small, a friend of a friend encouraged me to forgo purchasing coloring books for them. My initial reaction was one of horror. "What? Coloring books are fun! That would be forgoing fun! Plain paper? How boring!" Okay, granted… my reaction was a little melodramatic, but I do remember thinking these thoughts.

Instead, this friend insisted that providing children with blank sheets of paper was the way to spur creativity. I could see the wisdom. Not to mention, a ream of paper was way cheaper than four new coloring books… and so, I gave it a try. Does this mean I never gave my children coloring books? No! My children certainly enjoyed a few coloring books here and there. However, I admit that these books never seemed to offer my children the same kind of joy that coloring books had offered me. And so, for the most part, my children simply grew up with lots of plain white paper and a variety of colorful pencils, crayons, and markers.

PLAIN, WHITE PAPER IT WAS. What happened? My kids learned to draw. Not just little stick figures in the middle of the page, but they learned to tell a story using a piece of paper. Masterpieces. (So this mom deems them.)

Now, I'm sure no one ever saved one of my coloring book pages. Oh, for sure! Sometimes one landed on Grandma's refrigerator. However, right now, in my basement, there remain binders of pictures that my budding artists created twenty years ago.

Why? These pictures provide windows into their little souls and minds. For example, if God was not present in a Bible story, my son would draw a big eye in the sky. In his little five-year-old heart, he understood that God could see him. Had I handed my children coloring book pages where they filled in the blanks, I would never have had this window into their hearts and minds. Their works of art tell stories. And I treasure them in my heart.

THIS IS THE GIST OF **SIMPLY BIBLE**. These guides provide a "blank page" for reading and directly engaging with God and His Word. Rather than fill-in-the-blank questions, SIMPLY BIBLE offers space to be curious and ask your own questions. You will learn to observe, understand, and apply. Don't get me wrong: just like coloring books, traditional Bible studies have their place. Without them, I wouldn't be the Bible student that I am today. And yet, like many others, I am rather fond of this SIMPLY BIBLE series, offering a new way to engage directly with God. With gentle direction, these books allow quiet spaces for listening to and knowing God, relating with Him by sharing in His story: *simply the Bible.*

Since its inception, I've known the joy and privilege of watching others seek God through SIMPLY BIBLE. I've watched these Bible study journals become windows into hearts, souls, and minds growing with God. These workbooks tell personal stories. And although the stories are often much too private for me to observe closely, I treasure each one in my heart. If I could, I'd pile them up in my basement. Perhaps it's cheesy, but in some tender way, they all pile up in the "basement in my heart."

Finally, I want to thank Melissa Trew. SIMPLY BIBLE would not be the same without her. As a gifted designer, she takes an ordinary idea and transforms it into extraordinarily beautiful workbooks. Coffee-table-worthy. Melissa, I am eternally grateful. The longer we partner together in creating these studies, the more I appreciate you. From the bottom of my heart, thank you.

SO WELCOME TO **SIMPLY BIBLE**! The rest of the introduction provides step-by-step guidance on getting started with the inductive Bible study method. Please read these sections before beginning the study.

simply bible

AN INDUCTIVE BIBLE STUDY

After her first study, a friend described SIMPLY BIBLE as "leaving behind her paint by numbers set for a blank canvas." Whether painting, drawing, *or* digging into God's Word, using a blank canvas can be a little intimidating. It takes practice! Just as artists learn particular methods and handle special tools to create a masterpiece, so do Bible study students.

The methodology utilized within SIMPLY BIBLE is known as *inductive study*. This method is used by Bible scholars, pastors, teachers, and students of all levels, and can easily be completed using a Bible and plain notebook. Frankly, the SIMPLY BIBLE workbooks are not necessary for inductive study. However, most readers agree that these user-friendly guides simplify and ease the study process by providing everything needed in one place via an attractive, logical format.

The inductive method involves three basic steps that often overlap with one another:

(1) Observe
(2) Interpret
(3) Apply

This three-step format helps to paint a more thorough understanding of God's Word.

On the following pages, you will find A QUICK-START GUIDE TO **SIMPLY BIBLE**. Bookmark and use this as needed. The quick-start guide is followed by a more thorough explanation of the format and basic study tools. Take time to get a feel for each step. Read the examples. And then, dig in!

O GOD, YOU ARE MY GOD;
EARNESTLY I SEEK YOU...

PSALM 63:1

getting *started*

A QUICK-START GUIDE

getting *started*

A QUICK-START GUIDE

READ	OBSERVE	INTERPRET
Read the passage. Try some or all of these ideas to help you read carefully. (Highlighters and colored pencils are fun here!)	As you read, write down your observations in this column. Simply notice what the Scripture *says*. This is your place for notes. Ideas include:	In this column, record what the passage *means*.

Read the passage. Try some or all of these ideas to help you read carefully. (Highlighters and colored pencils are fun here!)

As you read, write down your observations in this column. Simply notice what the Scripture *says*. This is your place for notes. Ideas include:

In this column, record what the passage *means*.

One way to interpret is to answer any questions asked during observation. Try to first answer these *without* the aid of other helps. Allow Scripture to explain Scripture. It often does.

• Read the passage in a different version.

• Ask questions of the text, like "who, what, when, where, or how."

If the answers are not intuitive or easily found near the passage, other tools are available. Use boxes A, B, and C to identify a key word, define it, and look up a cross reference. This extra research will shed light on the meaning.

• Read it out loud.

• Jot down key items: people, places, things. Mark places on a map.

• Underline, circle, box, or highlight repeated words, unfamiliar words, or anything that pricks your heart or catches your attention.

• Ask, "What does this passage say about God? Jesus? Holy Spirit?"

IMPORTANT: *Seek to understand what Scripture meant to the psalmists (the authors of the Psalms) and to the original Hebrew readers (or hearers). Try to see and look at the world through the eyes of the Ancient Near East culture.*

• Note what took place before and after this passage.

• Listen to the passage while running errands.

• Ponder.

• Doodle or write out a verse in your workbook or a journaling Bible.

• Ask God if there is anything else He'd like you to notice.

PLEASE NOTE: The following boxes (labeled A, B, and C) are interpretation tools. These are meant to be used in unison with the "Interpret" column on the previous page to aid in interpreting Scripture. Most students find it helpful to complete these before interpreting. Consider this your toolbox. Use the tools that are most helpful for you.

A KEY WORDS	B DEFINITIONS	C CROSS REFERENCES
When you notice a word that is repeated multiple times, unfamiliar, or interesting to you in any other way, record it here.	Record definitions of your key words. You can find the appropriate definitions by using: • a Bible concordance (defines words according to the original language) • a Bible dictionary • another translation	Note cross references. This is a solid way to allow Scripture to interpret Scripture. If your Bible does not include cross references, they can be found easily using web-based Bible resources.

Bible study tools like those listed above can be found by visiting the following websites:

blueletterbible.org   **biblegateway.com**   **biblehub.com**

MAIN POINTS	APPLY
Summarize the main point(s) or note any themes you encountered in the passage.	Apply God's Word specifically to your own life. Application is personal. God may teach, correct, rebuke, or train. He is always equipping. (II Tim. 3:16-17) Record what the passage means to you.

PRAY

Write a short prayer here. When we take time to write something down, that message becomes more etched on our heart. Take a moment to simply be with God. He is why we study. Savor. Know. Praise. Confess. Thank. Ask. Love. Then carry a nugget of His Word in your heart to ponder and proclaim throughout your day.

BUT YOU, O LORD, ARE
A SHIELD ABOUT ME,
MY GLORY, AND THE
LIFTER OF MY HEAD.

PSALM 3:3

step by *step*

UNPACKING THE INDUCTIVE METHOD

step by *step*
UNPACKING THE INDUCTIVE METHOD

STEPS 1 & 2: READ AND OBSERVE | *See what the Bible* **says**.

The first step of Bible study is to observe God's Word.

In our hurried, scurried pace of life, we read too fast, often plowing through the words without taking time to ponder and think about what we're reading. *Observation* helps us to slow down and take notice in order to see. In this first step, we answer, "What does the Bible *say?*"

Have you ever stopped to truly examine and enjoy a piece of art? Artists develop an amazing knack or ability to capture a particular scene, whether real or imagined, onto a blank canvas. How? Artists specialize in observing details: setting, color, texture, time, characters, lighting, movement... The list of details is nearly limitless.

We can, too.

When my children were younger, blank sketch pads and new drawing pencils correlated to a special treat. With fresh, new artist tools in hand and a sunny day, my little ones and I would traipse excitedly through a park. Before pulling out a pencil to begin creating, we needed to find the right observation spot for observing. (I highly recommend that for Bible study, too!)

To observe means "to see, watch, notice, or regard with attention, especially so as to see or learn something."[1] *Especially so as to see or learn something.*

---

[1] **observe**. Dictionary.com. *Dictionary.com Unabridged.* Random House, Inc. http://www.dictionary.com/browse/observe (accessed: March 16, 2018).

And so, my children and I would notice things. Lots of things... the different types of leaves, flowers, plants, grass, insects, animals, and more. Once engaged in observing, details would begin to arise! How fun to zero in and observe the ladybug crawling along the blade of grass or the spots that adorn a toad sunning on the sidewalk or the veins that run throughout a maple leaf. There's so much to see!

Observation implies being curious. Noticing details. Asking questions.

Kids do this naturally. We can too. Be curious with God's Word. Scripture is full of details to notice and numerous questions to ask. When we slow down and take time to "smell the roses" within Scripture, we see and learn.

If you are not relating to creating art or being a kid again, then consider detective work. Inductive study is much like detective work. Detectives are trained to observe and notice details. They exude curiosity and examine cases by asking questions: who, what, when, where, how, and why.

Like detectives, we use observation skills too. Intuitively, without even thinking about it, we observe and interpret life around us.

Consider a family member or roommate. Using simple observation, we discern whether a loved one comes home happy, sad, or mad. After all, there's a huge difference between walking through the door with a smile or a frown. Singing a tune versus grumbling. Dancing versus slamming doors. We notice the "signs." And because we care, we ask questions. Inquisitive minds want to know, "What's up?" This leads to more questions: "Really? How? Why? Where? When? Who? Are you okay?" You get the picture.

Detective work transfers to reading and understanding God's Word. Observation means we read, study, and ask questions of the text. We look to see, "What does the Scripture say?" If short on time, we simply ask, "What does the Scripture say about who God is?"

As you read, pray and talk with God about His Word. Ask Him to help you see. Ask Him questions about the text. Highlight verses that touch your heart. If anything is especially noteworthy to you, jot it down in the space labeled **Observe** in your workbook. (Keep in mind: the SIMPLY BIBLE framework is just a guide. You can choose to fill in as little or as much as you desire.)

The bottom line? Read. Read carefully. Observe at least one thing, particularly something about God Himself. This allows us to see Scripture more clearly.

STEP 3: INTERPRET | *Understand what the Bible **means**.*

After careful observation of a landscape, an artist sketches an interpretation of what he sees onto the canvas. Observation and interpretation go hand in hand. A circle is a circle. A square is a square. As closely as possible, the artist defines and places an image of what he observes onto the canvas. Careful observation leads to a life-like rendering such that the viewer will understand what the artist himself observed.

The same is true of the Bible. Observation and interpretation go hand in hand. Scripture will often interpret Scripture. As we carefully read and observe what the Scripture says, we frequently understand and simultaneously interpret its *meaning*. So within our daily study format, observation and interpretation are located side-by-side.

One simple way to understand the meaning of Scripture is to answer the questions we asked in the observation process: the who, what, where, when, how, and why. Try to answer these questions without the aid of study notes or other helps. Utilize Scripture to interpret Scripture. Often, the answer is readily available.

Other times, interpretation is not so easy. After all, the Bible was written in ancient times, spanning the course of over two thousand years, *by* a people and *to* a people of a culture that is utterly foreign to us.

Therefore, certain resources are handy. These tools can help us to place and understand Scripture in its original context in order to properly interpret. (Think of an artist using a ruler—a simple tool that helps to more accurately reproduce a scene. A ruler is not necessary, but is useful.)

Bible study tools can include:

- *Cross references:* Cross references allow us to use nearby or related passages to more accurately interpret Scripture.
- *Bible dictionaries or concordances:* These tools allow students to understand the meaning of a word in its original language.
- *Bible handbooks and commentaries:* Resources like these help us to verify our conclusions as well as provide historical or cultural context.

It's important to remember that Scripture, in its original context, had only one meaning. Not multiple meanings. And although our God can be mysterious in His ways, there are no mystical or hidden meanings within Scripture. The Psalms echo cries of the heart! The psalmist wrote a specific song, with a specific message, at a specific time, and in a specific place, for a specific person or group of people. He meant what he said.

For this study, we want to know what a psalmist meant and how the Hebrews of the Ancient Near East understood his words. Although we may not always be able to determine a psalmist's specific intent, that is our goal. Additionally, in the case of wisdom literature, understanding how Jesus and the 1st century Jews interpreted the Psalms is also insightful. Interpretation implies understanding. Original meaning and context are important.

Seek correct answers, but give yourself grace. A child's rendering of a ladybug on a blade of grass will not equate to Van Gogh's renderings, and yet, there is something wholly precious about the works of a child. Our renderings of Scripture won't ever equate to a Bible scholar's commentary. That is not our goal. Our goal is knowing God. Sometimes this involves taking tiny baby steps in His direction.

A, B, & C: TOOLS FOR INTERPRETATION

If the answers are not intuitive or easily found within the passage, tools are available to help us better understand. Our daily lesson format provides three boxes intended to support interpretation. Here, you'll find space to identify key words, define those key words, and record supporting verses (cross references). These are intended to help and guide you as you interpret Scripture. Consider this to be your interpretation toolbox. Use the tools however you find them to be helpful.

A. KEY WORDS | Did you notice that a word was repeated, seems important, is unfamiliar, or interests you in any way? Record it here.

B. DEFINITIONS | Use this box to record definitions of the words you listed.

• *Read the verse using a different translation or version of the Bible.* This can be a very simple way to define a word. For example, our practice lesson (on page 32) notes the word *extol* from Psalm 117 because this is not a word we use every day. The ESV version says "extol," while the New Living Translation says: "praise." The Message uses "applaud."[1]

• *Use a Bible concordance.* This book looks at words in their original language. I like the **Strong's Concordance**, which can also be found online.

   i. Going online? Try **Blue Letter Bible** at **blueletterbible.org.**

   ii. Once there, (referring to our practice lesson on page 32) simply type "Psalm 117" into the *Search the Bible* box. Select the box called *Tools* and a menu appears. Find and select the corresponding Strong's Concordance number for "apostle" (in this case: H7643). You'll retrieve the Greek word, original definitions, and where else it is used in Scripture. It's fascinating!

---

[1] Peterson, Eugene H. *The Message: The Bible in Contemporary Language.* NavPress, 2002.

- *Try a Bible dictionary.* In order to define people or locate places, Bible dictionaries are handy.

  i. Online, try **Bible Gateway, Blue Letter Bible,** or **Bible Hub** for free.

  ii. There are also wonderful apps available for you to use, including **Bible Map.** This simple-to-use app automatically syncs Scripture with maps.

C. CROSS REFERENCES | Many Bibles offer cross references. This is a rock-solid way to allow Scripture to interpret Scripture. If your Bible does not include cross references (most journaling Bibles do not), no worries! Accessing cross references online is easy. **Blue Letter Bible** or **Bible Hub** are great places to start.

Still not sure?

Note your question and talk to God about it. Ponder. As we ponder Scripture, God often illuminates our understanding. Other times, He allows certain things to remain unanswered. His ways are sometimes beyond our ways and our understanding. We walk by faith.

Remember to share and discuss your questions with others at Bible study. Studying God's Word is meant to be done in community where we learn and grow together in knowing, understanding, and loving God.

WANT MORE? Our daily study format includes space for definitions and cross references. However, there are other Bible study resources available if you'd like to dig even deeper.

Bible commentaries are written by Biblical scholars. These books provide cultural and historical context while commenting on Scripture verse-by-verse.

Personally, I admire the dedication and genius of scholars who write commentaries. These dedicated people study for the glory of God. And yet, I recommend saving their wonderful resources as a last step. Why? Because commentaries are not a substitute for reading, understanding, and engaging God's Word on your own. First seek to understand God's Word without a commentary. Then, if desired, utilize a commentary for double-checking your work.

Also, please note that commentaries are written according to various theological bents. It's helpful to compare. Know your sources. This is especially crucial if roaming the Internet. Please surf with discernment and great care. I can't emphasize this enough. Unfortunately, even commentaries found on popular Bible study sites are not always researched or written by trained Biblical scholars. If unsure, background-check the author's credentials. Bible degrees and scholastic training from accredited universities and institutions are important.

To find reliable Biblical commentaries, I recommend:

www.bestcommentary.com   **www.challies.com**

SUMMARIZE: Your daily framework offers space for you to summarize and identify the main point(s) of the Bible passage you've read. Understanding the main idea of a passage helps to ensure a correct interpretation before moving into application.

STEP 4: APPLY | *Put it all **together**.*

Here's the "So what? How will I think or act differently because of God's Word?"

With the Holy Spirit's help, observation and interpretation lead us to better understand the meaning of a Bible passage. That's thrilling! Discovering a nugget of truth, a promise or a revelation about God Himself takes my breath away and inevitably leads me to praise and worship Him. There is no other book like the Bible:

> For the word of God is living and active,
> sharper than any two-edged sword,
> piercing to the division of soul and of spirit,
> of joints and of marrow, and discerning
> the thoughts and intentions of the heart.
>
> HEBREWS 4:12

The God of the Universe loves us and reveals Himself through His Living Word. When He does, it cuts in a good way. Then we're ready to apply His Word to our everyday lives. This is where God does His transforming work to help us *think* and *live* differently.

APPLICATION IS THE CREATIVE PART. Yes, the original author of Scripture had one meaning, but the personal applications of Scripture are many. This step is between you and God. If a specific verse, word, or idea strikes a chord in your heart, *slow down*. Take note. Show God the discovery. This is the amazing process of God revealing Himself and His truths to you through His Word and the power of His Spirit.

God looks at our hearts. He sees, knows, and loves His sheep. And so, He may use His Word to teach, correct, rebuke, or train. He is always equipping (II Timothy 3:16-17). If you're willing, He will lead you to apply His Word specifically to your everyday life.

Application ideas include:
1 | Worship God for who He is, according to a truth or promise discovered.
2 | Thank Him for a lesson learned.
3 | Note an example to follow.
4 | Confess a sin revealed.
5 | Pray a prayer noticed.
6 | Obey, trust, and follow God's way, His command, His plan.
7 | Memorize a verse.

Bottom line? Ask yourself, "How will I think or act differently because of what I've learned in God's Word?"

WRAPPING UP: PRAY | *Respond to a **Holy God**.*

Application implies a recognition of who God is. And so, when wrapping up personal study, the application step almost always leads me to bow my heart in worship, confession, or thanksgiving. Hence, the SIMPLY BIBLE daily format includes a place for *prayer*. Please use this! It may be the most important space of all.

Enjoy a lingering moment of being with God in His Word. Savor. Learn. Grow. Know. Thank. Praise. Confess. Yield. Love. Then carry a nugget of truth in your heart to ponder as you go about your day.

lesson *samples*

PRACTICE LESSONS & EXAMPLES

practice *lesson*

PSALM 117

NOW IT'S YOUR TURN! Give it a try! Below is a short, two-verse psalm of praise: Psalm 117. As you read, feel free to highlight, circle, underline, and mark up the text in whatever way you like. In the *Observe* column, jot down details that pop out and write down questions that come to mind. Then *Interpret*. Simply use the Scripture itself or hop over to the toolkit of *Key Words*, *Definitions*, and *Cross References*. Use these as previously discussed to help you better understand the meaning. Finish by summarizing, applying, and praying.

This is your workbook. Simply journal your thoughts as you engage with God and His Word. Don't be shy...

READ

¹ Praise the LORD, all nations!
   Extol him, all peoples!
² For great is his steadfast love toward us,
   and the faithfulness of the LORD endures forever.
Praise the LORD!

OBSERVE	INTERPRET

KEY WORDS	DEFINITIONS	CROSS REFERENCES

MAIN POINT(S)

APPLY

PRAY

sample *lesson*

PSALM 117 | FOR THOSE CRAZY, BUSY DAYS

We're busy. Life can be hectic. Some days, you may not have time to go deep in your study. That's okay. One truth from God's Word transforms hearts which often transforms the day. Using Psalm 117, here's what a study might look like with very little time. The goal is to observe, interpret, and apply just *one* thing (particularly about who God is):

READ

¹ Praise the LORD, all nations!
    Extol him, all peoples!
² For great is his steadfast love toward us,
    and the faithfulness of the LORD endures forever.
Praise the LORD!

OBSERVE

The LORD is mentioned 3 times. What does the psalmist say about Him?

INTERPRET

Praise the Lord - 2x.

Extol Him.

His steadfast love toward us is great.

The faithfulness of the Lord endures forever.

KEY WORDS	DEFINITIONS	CROSS REFERENCES
extol	praise *(New Living Translation)*; applaud *(The Message)*	

MAIN POINT(S)

This psalm calls all people to praise the Lord.

APPLY

The main goal of the psalmist seems to be praising God and encouraging others to praise God. Is praising and applauding God even on my own To-Do List today?

PRAY

Lord God, the psalmist is right. All the nations and all the peoples should praise you! This psalm reminds me that you love me. I realize that in the midst of this crazy day, praising you was not even on my radar. I'm sorry. Please forgive me. Put Your praise on my lips and Your song in my heart.

sample *lesson*

PSALM 117 | GOING DEEPER

Do you have time to linger in God's Word? Using Psalm 117, here's an example of what a more extensive study could look like. Observe as much or as little as you like. Remember: No two journals will look the same. This is yours. Mark it up, draw, and use it however you like.

READ

¹ Praise the LORD, all nations!
    Extol him, all peoples!
² For great is his steadfast love toward us,
    and the faithfulness of the LORD endures forever.
Praise the LORD!

OBSERVE	INTERPRET
The LORD is mentioned 3 times. What does the psalmist say about Him?	Praise the Lord - 2x.
Praise - 2x	Extol Him.
Why is *Lord* in all caps?	His steadfast love toward us is great.
What does *extol* mean? Is it the same as *praise*, since it's found in the second cola?	The faithfulness of the Lord endures forever.
What does it mean for something to endure forever?	

KEY WORDS	DEFINITIONS	CROSS REFERENCES
extol	praise (New Living Translation); applaud (The Message)	Romans 15:11 And again, "Praise the Lord, all you Gentiles, and let all the peoples extol him."
LORD	Yahweh	
Steadfast love	Loyal love, kindness, mercy (hesed)	Psalm 103:11 For as high as the heavens are above the earth, so great is his steadfast love toward those who fear him...
Faithfulness	Firmness, trustworthy, constancy	
Endures forever	Everlasting, perpetual, ancient, evermore	Psalm 100:5 For the LORD is good; his steadfast love endures forever, and his faithfulness to all generations.

MAIN POINT(S)

This psalm calls all people to praise the Lord because of His love and faithfulness that endures forever.

APPLY

The main goal of the psalmist seems to be praising God and encouraging others to praise God. Is praising and applauding God even on my own To-Do List today? Practice praising God!

PRAY

Lord God, the psalmist is right. All the nations and all the peoples should praise you! This psalm reminds me that you love me, constantly, faithfully. I'm reminded that you will never stop loving me and I am safe with you. Lord, I realize that in the midst of this crazy day, praising you was not even on my radar. I'm sorry. Please forgive me. Put Your praise on my lips and Your song in my heart for this day! I praise You for Your constant love that endures forever!

YOU DID IT! That's it. That's all there is to the SIMPLY BIBLE inductive process. If this is your first time, the process may feel a little awkward at first. Don't worry. You probably don't remember how clumsy and time-consuming it was the very first time you tried tying your shoe, riding a bike, or driving a car. Practice helps. The same will be true for Bible study. Like riding a bicycle, it gets easier.

Likewise, please know that your study guide will look different from most others. You are unique and special. And so, your observations and application will be unique. Every artist creates something different with her "blank page."

Indeed, you've probably gathered by now that this study is different. And different often falls outside our comfort zones. The purpose of this Bible study is that you may confidently read, understand, and apply God's Word like never before, using *simply the Bible*.

IT REQUIRES A COMMITMENT. Would you please commit to finishing this study book? By the end, with consistency, perseverance, and time spent with Him, you will better know God, His Word, and your identity in Him.

You're more observant, smarter, and stronger than you think you are. God created you that way. He desires to be known. He wants to show you that you are loved, valued, and never alone. So lean into Him; ask, seek, and you will find. His grace is sufficient. His power is made perfect in our weakness.

As the rain and the snow come down from heaven,
and do not return to it without watering the earth
and making it bud and flourish,
so that it yields seed for the sower and bread for the eater,

so is my word that goes out from my mouth:
It will not return to me empty,
but will accomplish what I desire
and achieve the purpose for which I sent it.

You will go out in joy and be led forth in peace;
the mountains and hills will burst into song before you,
and all the trees of the field will clap their hands.

ISAIAH 55:10-12

Lord God Almighty, Thank You for Your Word! Like rain and snow watering the earth so that it might bud and flourish, may Your Word now water our hearts, minds, and souls, that our love for You and for one another would bud and flourish. May Your purposes and desires be accomplished. As we study with You, may we go out in joy and be led forth in Your peace. With all creation may we sing and clap for joy and bring glory to Your Name...

HE LEADS ME BESIDE
STILL WATERS. HE
RESTORES MY SOUL.

PSALM 23:2-3

in *context*

EXAMINING THE CONTEXT OF **PSALMS**

in *context*

EXAMINING THE CONTEXT OF **PSALMS**

GENRE

The book of Psalms belongs to a genre of the Bible known as *Wisdom Literature*, which also includes the books of Job, Proverbs, Ecclesiastes, and the Song of Songs (Song of Solomon). To the Hebrews, "wisdom" constituted "skill in living." Israel's wisdom literature utilized poetry and was shaped not only by an intense faith in the Lord, but also by an innate desire to celebrate the worth and meaning of human existence. Hebrew poetry offered a higher vehicle for theologizing or studying God, while simultaneously allowing the literature to be more readily accessible to God's people. For a culture that was mostly illiterate, this was important.

Sometimes referred to as Israel's hymn book, Psalms likewise provides a distinct window into Old Testament theology. The prayers exude great trust in an Almighty God who reigns sovereign over His people, a God who sees, knows, understands, and provides. A God who is worthy of worship. With passionate faith, the prayers of the psalmist often reveal the intensity of both human existence and human emotions. The book of Psalms represents the honest cries and joys of God's people before the Lord.

Timeless. Transcendent. Not bound to the ancient historical context, this song book of the Bible continues to provide wisdom for daily living, walking, and talking with God. The heart cries of the psalmist resonate with and give words to our own heart cries. Perhaps this helps to explain why the psalms remain some of the most popular literature of the Bible, even today.

AUTHORSHIP & DATE

For the most part, scholars do not know a lot about who wrote the psalms or how to date them. The complete collection of Israel's songbook includes psalms written from the time of Moses to the post-exilic period, that period of Jewish history between the end of the exile in Babylon in 538 BC and AD 1. In other words, this book is made up of poems written during a vast one-thousand-year period! The final edition was formatted sometime after the Babylonian exile and before the time of Christ.

Authorship of the various psalms may be determined by the titles and the superscriptions — those brief, narrative statements in the beginning of certain psalms that stand outside the actual text. Once again, scholars aren't sure when to date the superscriptions. These themselves are very old and most likely come from the editorial process in order to help place the psalm in context. Some scholars even disagree on whether or not the psalms that reference David are actually written by David or if these were written for or to him. However, New Testament quotes typically point to David's authorship. For example, Luke records Jesus saying:

> For David himself says in the Book of Psalms,
> "'The Lord said to my Lord,
> "Sit at my right hand,
> until I make your enemies your footstool."'"
>
> LUKE 20:42-43

No matter what, out of Moses, Asaph, sons of Korah, and others, David remains the psalter's number-one influencer. In fact, 73 of the psalms refer to him in some way, with 13 of them being linked to a particular narrative context. The Dead Sea scrolls suggest that David himself composed 3,600 psalms, while the Jewish Talmud attributes the entire psalter to David. Although not the only author included in this book, David's heart shines through a study of the Psalms.

ORGANIZATION & TITLE

These psalms were gradually collected and compiled into Israel's hymnbook, and so, we need to distinguish between the *editor* of the book of Psalms and the various *authors* of the individual psalms. The editor (or editors) divided the 150 psalms into five books:

Introduction | Psalm 1-2 *(a wisdom and a royal psalm set the stage for the psalter)*
Book 1 | Psalms 3-41
Book 2 | Psalms 42-72
Book 3 | Psalms 73-89
Book 4 | Psalms 90-106
Book 5 | Psalms 107-145 *(praise)*
Conclusion | Psalms 146-150 *(strong praise songs)*

Traditionally, this collection of songs was untitled, but associated with the Hebrew words for prayer and praise. The book gained the English name, "Psalms," from the Greek *psal-moi*, which refers to songs of praise and their lyrics. The inclusion of Psalms into the whole canon of scripture remains non-controversial. Jesus, himself, spoke of the Psalms:

> Then he said to them, "These are my words that I spoke to you while I was still with you, that every-thing written about me in the Law of Moses and the Prophets and the Psalms must be fulfilled."
>
> LUKE 24:44

HEBREW POETRY

For a study of Psalms, it's helpful to know a bit about Hebrew poetry. Hebrew poetry is not full of rhyming words and meter, as is characteristic of modern English poetry. And even when it is, we miss the beauty of the unique alliteration, sound, and grammar, due to the translation from Hebrew to our own language. However, one exceptional and critical feature of Hebrew poetry sparkles despite translation: *parallelism*.

PARALLELISM: Parallelism exists **when two phrases of poetry relate or correspond to one another.** Psalm 95:1-5 clearly demonstrates the relationship or correspondence between the groups of two phrases:

> ¹ Oh come, let us sing to the LORD;
>   let us make a joyful noise to the rock of our salvation!
> ² Let us come into his presence with thanksgiving;
>   let us make a joyful noise to him with songs of praise!
> ³ For the LORD is a great God,
>   and a great King above all gods.
> ⁴ In his hand are the depths of the earth;
>   the heights of the mountains are his also.
> ⁵ The sea is his, for he made it,
>   and his hands formed the dry land.
>
> PSALM 95:1-5

Did you notice the relationship or correspondence in meaning between the first and second phrases of each verse? The Hebrew parallelism shines. In his book *Reflections on the Psalms*, C. S. Lewis gives a quick definition of parallelism as "the practice of saying twice the same thing in different words." [1] But really, the second phrase is saying something similar *and* something different. A good question for the purposes of our study is, "How is the second phrase (cola B) different?"

For ease of discussion, let's briefly examine terms used to identify various parts of Hebrew poetry, from the smallest to the largest parts:

COLON: one phrase or line of poetry, a subunit of a line.

Example:
The LORD is my shepherd; *(Psalm 23:1)*

---

[1] Lewis, C.S. (1958). *Reflections on the Psalms.* (p.3). New York: Harcourt, Brace, Jovanovich.

COLA: the plural of colon. There can be: bi-colon, tri-colon, quatrain, mono-colon.

Example of bi-colon:
The LORD is my shepherd;
    I shall not want. *(Psalm 23:1)*

Example of tri-colon:
Even though I walk through the valley of the shadow of death,
    I will fear no evil,
    for you are with me; *(Psalm 23:4)*

LINE: a unit comprised of one or more cola. Lines are usually distinguished in the Bible text by indentation. (Single-column editions of the Bible are best when reading Hebrew poetry. As much as possible, this SIMPLY BIBLE study seeks to utilize the single column format.)

Example:
The LORD is my shepherd; I shall not want. *(Psalm 23:1)*

STROPHES: Groups of closely-related lines, similar to a paragraph.

STANZAS: Closely-related groups of strophes.

MUSICAL MARKINGS: Some psalms contain musical markings. Similar to superscriptions, these descriptions are outside of the text and not read as part of the psalm. Several psalms include a liturgical title related to public worship. Others include:

"For the director of music:" Over fifty psalms have this title, and there is a general consensus that the psalms were entrusted to the care of the person in charge of worship at the sanctuary.

"Tunes:" A number of phrases appear in the titles to refer to the tune of the song. These tunes have been lost over time.

"Voices and instruments:" Some of the technical terms in the titles seem to call for certain types of musical accompaniment, instruments, or singing.

SELAH: This term occurs a little over 70 times in the psalms, typically at the end of a poetic line. Some believe it marks a kind of interlude, although the few times when it appears in the middle of a thought argues against that interpretation (see Psalm 68:7–8 as an example). [1]

IMAGERY

Along with parallelism, imagery breathes life into the Psalms. As William Brown has put it, "The power of Psalms lies first and foremost in its evocative use of language." That is, the power of the psalms to touch people's lives flows from the way the psalter uses metaphor, simile, hyperbole, imagery, drama, intensity, repetition, and so on. [2]

Imagery is the use of various word pictures throughout a poem; the language used that appeals to our five senses of seeing, hearing, smelling, tasting, and touching. The ancient imagery of Hebrew poetry employs concrete images from everyday life. But these images from an ancient world are very different from our 21st-century world. For our study, we will need to investigate the ancient world of the Hebrews in order to better understand their images and word pictures.

At times the psalmist's images emote strong feelings, even cursing one's enemies. These instances shock our senses. As mentioned earlier in the introduction, we are not used to being honest with God. Keep in mind, the psalms are not meant to be read or studied

---

[1] Longman, T., III. (2014). *Psalms: An Introduction and Commentary.* (D. G. Firth, Ed.) (Vol. 15–16, p. 31). Nottingham, England: Inter-Varsity Press.

[2] deClaissé-Walford, N., Jacobson, R. A., & Tanner, B. L. (2014). *The Book of Psalms.* (E. J. Young, R. K. Harrison, & R. L. Hubbard Jr., Eds.) (p. 42). Grand Rapids, MI; Cambridge, U.K.: William B. Eerdmans Publishing Company.

literally. The genre is poetry. Rather, the psalms use figurative language and present word pictures to portray the psalmist's feelings. The psalmist does *not* act on his feelings, but honestly presents his emotions to God, doing the best he can to identify and give words to them. He surrenders both the crisis and his feelings *about* the crisis to the Lord, placing his trust and confidence in a Lord that knows his heart and has his best interest in mind, a Lord that saves and provides with wisdom and righteousness beyond man.

Imagery touches emotions and engages minds. We feel, and then we think. Everything we feel is found in one psalm or another. John Calvin says this:

> What various and resplendent riches are contained in this treasury, it were difficult to find words to describe.... I have been wont to call this book not inappropriately, an anatomy of all parts of the soul; for there is not an emotion of which any one can be conscious that is not here represented as in a mirror.
>
> JOHN CALVIN

Upon entering into someone else's hurt, pain and doubts, the reader connects to the psalm in a unique way. This connection requires not just our brains, but our hearts, too, where the psalms lead us to deep, dark places, places of transparency. Life is not so simple. And these prayers encourage us that God himself is *big enough!* Whatever we're experiencing, the imagery of the Psalms lets us know that it's okay. We can come just as we are and approach Him in the midst of our struggle.

This Hebrew prayer book offers us a glimpse of the closeness that God desires to have with us. This made sense to the ancient Israelites. It makes sense today. Even more so. For as we approach the Lord through the Psalms, we have the added assurance that God Himself has become the answer for us via His Son, Jesus Christ.

I SOUGHT THE LORD,
AND HE ANSWERED ME
AND DELIVERED ME
FROM ALL MY FEARS.

PSALM 34:4

TYPES OF PSALMS

Most psalms can be assigned into one of three categories: lament, thanksgiving, or praise. Lament psalms involve honestly seeking God in the midst of pain. Psalms of thanksgiving acknowledge God's faithfulness and provision in some way. And praise psalms worship and admire God for who He is.

Each type of psalm can be identified by specific characteristics or patterns. For our inductive study, let's familiarize ourselves with these three main types of psalms.

PSALMS OF LAMENT: Psalms of lament make up a third of all the psalms. Surprised? This is cause for celebration! The sheer number of lament psalms demonstrates that it really *is* okay to bring our sorrows, frustrations, anxieties, and shame to the Lord!

Lament psalms are generally marked by uncertainty in the midst of a crisis. The pain of the psalmist is very real, and his psalm teaches us how to transparently engage with God. The lament shows us that there is meaning in suffering. The psalmist *affirms* suffering; he does not simply jump to praise. In a lament psalm, the reader is called to move through the suffering with the psalmist until he eventually arrives to a place of trust in the Lord. The psalmist knows that when we have a hurt, we have recourse and can approach the Lord with boldness. This genre of psalm includes both **individual** and **communal laments**.

Psalms of lament typically follow this pattern (although not necessarily in this order):

1 | **Opening address:** In this vocative, the psalmist cries out to God.

2 | **Description of the plight or complaint:** The psalmist plainly describes the crisis.

3 | **Petition or plea for help:** The psalmist asks God for help.

4 | **Profession of trust in the Lord:** The psalmist declares his confidence in the Lord.

5 | **Pledge or vow to praise:** The psalmist promises to praise the Lord and perhaps even present a thanks offering.

PRAISE PSALMS: Praise or hymn psalms are very theocentric or God-centered. These form another twenty percent of the psalms, and generally, these psalms are found in the second half of the psalter. The pattern of praise psalms looks like this:

1 | **Invitation to praise:** The psalmist may give others an invitation or imperative command to praise.

2 | **Rationale or reason for praise:** God's character, glory, and power offer reasons for singing this hymn to Him.

3 | **Renewed call to praise:** A renewed call can be or is nearly a repeat of the first invitation to praise the Lord.

THANKSGIVING PSALMS: Thanksgiving psalms thank the Lord. It's that simple! Whether from an individual or communal crisis, these psalms almost always describe the Lord's rescue and sometimes recount historical events. Usually these psalms include:

1 | **Desire to thank Yahweh:** The psalmist offers to bless or thank the Lord.

2 | **Description of the crisis in narrative form:** The psalmist provides his reason for thanking the Lord and describes the Lord's good and faithful work or provision.

3 | **Conclusion:** The psalm may be concluded in a number of ways.

Scholars often break these three categories of psalms into more categories and sometimes even sub-categories, such as:

- **wisdom songs**
- **songs of trust**
- **pilgrim psalms**
- **royal psalms**
- **historical psalms**

Categories can vary by scholar and are not set in stone. Also the more categories, the more some psalms will overlap categories.

Our study is organized by the following categories:

WISDOM: Wisdom psalms are not necessarily connected to specific acts of worship and are essentially meditations on the good life.[1] These psalms provide instruction and contrast good versus evil, righteousness versus unrighteousness, or wise versus foolish.

ROYAL: The royal psalms emphasize kingship. Typically, the king is the central focus. Royal psalms may also include messianic overtones, ultimately pointing to the kingship of Christ.

LAMENT: Laments present a psalmist's cry to God when in distress and are marked by uncertainty in the midst of crisis. See pg. 50 for the traits characteristic of lament psalms.

COMMUNAL LAMENT: A communal lament includes all of the traits common to a lament psalm, but is representative of the *community* of Israel, rather than an individual.

PENITENTIAL: Casting oneself upon the Lord, the psalmist uses the penitential psalms to express remorse and seek the Lord's mercy and forgiveness.

TRUST: Psalms of trust express the psalmist's confidence in God's power and goodness.

PILGRIM: These hymns most likely were sung by worshippers as they journeyed toward or approached Jerusalem and the temple. Pilgrim psalms can involve a variety of genres, including lament, wisdom, trust, and thanksgiving.

THANKSGIVING: These psalms thank God for specific answers to prayer and acts of deliverance. They bear witness or testimony to God's good work in the psalmist's life.

---

[1] Bernhard W. Anderson, Steven Bishop. *Out of the Depths: The Psalms Speak for Us Today.* (Louisville, Kentucky: Westminster John Knox Press, 2000), 189.

PRAISE: Praise hymns are used to worship and praise God for His character, His glory, His power, and His sovereignty in creation, history, and redemption.

Because a psalm is meant to be read in its entirety, our study comprises one whole psalm per day. In order to stay true to the original format of each Psalm and to best highlight the parallelism found in Hebrew poetry, we've chosen to print the Psalms in one column. The SIMPLY BIBLE format for this book has been slightly modified to accommodate for these needs. Compared to other SIMPLY BIBLE studies, you may notice even more white space. Enjoy!

BECOME A PSALMIST! The Psalms are ready for personal use! At the end of each week's study, you'll find space in your workbook to journal your thoughts freely, to hand-letter Scripture verses creatively, or even to experiment with writing your own psalms to the Lord. See this not as a homework assignment or another checkbox on your "to-do list," but as a fresh way to lay your heart bare before the Lord and offer Him whatever new song He might inspire you to sing!

THE LAW OF THE LORD IS PERFECT,
REVIVING THE SOUL...

PSALM 19:7

chapter *one*

WISDOM PSALMS

take *note*

WISDOM PSALMS

take *note*

WISDOM PSALMS

day *one*

PSALM 1

READ

[1] Blessed is the man
   who walks not in the counsel of the wicked,
nor stands in the way of sinners,
   nor sits in the seat of scoffers;
[2] but his delight is in the law of the Lord,
   and on his law he meditates day and night.

[3] He is like a tree
   planted by streams of water
that yields its fruit in its season,
   and its leaf does not wither.
In all that he does, he prospers.
[4] The wicked are not so,
   but are like chaff that the wind drives away.

[5] Therefore the wicked will not stand in the judgment,
   nor sinners in the congregation of the righteous;
[6] for the Lord knows the way of the righteous,
   but the way of the wicked will perish.

OBSERVE	INTERPRET

KEY WORDS	DEFINITIONS	CROSS REFERENCES

MAIN POINT(S)	APPLY

PRAY

day *two*

PSALM 19

READ

¹ The heavens declare the glory of God,
　　and the sky above proclaims his handiwork.
² Day to day pours out speech,
　　and night to night reveals knowledge.
³ There is no speech, nor are there words,
　　whose voice is not heard.
⁴ Their voice goes out through all the earth,
　　and their words to the end of the world.
In them he has set a tent for the sun,
⁵　　which comes out like a bridegroom leaving his chamber,
　　and, like a strong man, runs its course with joy.
⁶ Its rising is from the end of the heavens,
　　and its circuit to the end of them,
　　and there is nothing hidden from its heat.

⁷ The law of the Lord is perfect,
　　reviving the soul;
the testimony of the Lord is sure,
　　making wise the simple;
⁸ the precepts of the Lord are right,
　　rejoicing the heart;
the commandment of the Lord is pure,
　　enlightening the eyes;
⁹ the fear of the Lord is clean,
　　enduring forever;
the rules of the Lord are true,
　　and righteous altogether.
¹⁰ More to be desired are they than gold,
　　even much fine gold;
sweeter also than honey

---

and drippings of the honeycomb.
¹¹ Moreover, by them is your servant warned;
in keeping them there is great reward.

¹² Who can discern his errors?
Declare me innocent from hidden faults.
¹³ Keep back your servant also from presumptuous sins;
let them not have dominion over me!
Then I shall be blameless,
and innocent of great transgression.

¹⁴ Let the words of my mouth and the meditation of my heart
be acceptable in your sight,
O Lord, my rock and my redeemer.

OBSERVE

INTERPRET

KEY WORDS	DEFINITIONS	CROSS REFERENCES

MAIN POINT(S)

APPLY

PRAY

day *three*

PSALM 49

READ

[1] Hear this, all peoples!
    Give ear, all inhabitants of the world,
[2] both low and high,
    rich and poor together!
[3] My mouth shall speak wisdom;
    the meditation of my heart shall be understanding.
[4] I will incline my ear to a proverb;
    I will solve my riddle to the music of the lyre.

[5] Why should I fear in times of trouble,
    when the iniquity of those who cheat me surrounds me,
[6] those who trust in their wealth
    and boast of the abundance of their riches?
[7] Truly no man can ransom another,
    or give to God the price of his life,
[8] for the ransom of their life is costly
    and can never suffice,
[9] that he should live on forever
    and never see the pit.

[10] For he sees that even the wise die;
    the fool and the stupid alike must perish
    and leave their wealth to others.
[11] Their graves are their homes forever,
    their dwelling places to all generations,
    though they called lands by their own names.
[12] Man in his pomp will not remain;
    he is like the beasts that perish.

---

¹³ This is the path of those who have foolish confidence;
  yet after them people approve of their boasts. *Selah*
¹⁴ Like sheep they are appointed for Sheol;
  death shall be their shepherd,
and the upright shall rule over them in the morning.
  Their form shall be consumed in Sheol, with no place to dwell.
¹⁵ But God will ransom my soul from the power of Sheol,
  for he will receive me. *Selah*

¹⁶ Be not afraid when a man becomes rich,
  when the glory of his house increases.
¹⁷ For when he dies he will carry nothing away;
  his glory will not go down after him.
¹⁸ For though, while he lives, he counts himself blessed
  —and though you get praise when you do well for yourself—
¹⁹ his soul will go to the generation of his fathers,
  who will never again see light.
²⁰ Man in his pomp yet without understanding is like the beasts that perish.

OBSERVE	INTERPRET

KEY WORDS	DEFINITIONS	CROSS REFERENCES

MAIN POINT(S)

APPLY

PRAY

day *four*

PSALM 112

READ

¹ Praise the Lord!
Blessed is the man who fears the Lord,
  who greatly delights in his commandments!
² His offspring will be mighty in the land;
  the generation of the upright will be blessed.
³ Wealth and riches are in his house,
  and his righteousness endures forever.
⁴ Light dawns in the darkness for the upright;
  he is gracious, merciful, and righteous.
⁵ It is well with the man who deals generously and lends;
  who conducts his affairs with justice.
⁶ For the righteous will never be moved;
  he will be remembered forever.
⁷ He is not afraid of bad news;
  his heart is firm, trusting in the Lord.
⁸ His heart is steady; he will not be afraid,
  until he looks in triumph on his adversaries.
⁹ He has distributed freely; he has given to the poor;
  his righteousness endures forever;
  his horn is exalted in honor.
¹⁰ The wicked man sees it and is angry;
  he gnashes his teeth and melts away;
  the desire of the wicked will perish!

OBSERVE	INTERPRET

KEY WORDS	DEFINITIONS	CROSS REFERENCES

MAIN POINT(S)

APPLY

PRAY

day *five*

1 Summarize what you learned from this week's wisdom psalms.	2 Which psalm or verse was your favorite? Explain.
3 Did you notice any common themes or elements in these wisdom psalms?	4 To the Hebrews, wisdom represented "skill in living." In light of this, what favorite instruction did you find this week?
5 According to these psalms, define *wicked*.	6 What stands out to you concerning the ways of the wicked? Are you convicted in any way?

7 Accordingly, define *righteous*.

8 What stands out to you concerning the ways of the righteous?

9 Practically, how will you apply one "righteous" example from these psalms?

10 Sometimes wisdom psalms include beatitudes ("Blessed is the one who…"). Can you find an example? What does it mean to be "blessed?"

11 What did you learn about God through these wisdom psalms?

12 What did you learn about how to worship God?

take it to *heart*

USE THIS SPACE TO WRITE OUT OR JOURNAL A FAVORITE VERSE FROM THIS WEEK'S STUDY, OR WRITE OUT YOUR OWN WISDOM PSALM. (THIS IS BETWEEN YOU AND GOD.)

SERVE THE LORD WITH FEAR,
AND REJOICE WITH TREMBLING.

PSALM 2:11

chapter *two*

ROYAL PSALMS

take *note*

ROYAL PSALMS

take *note*

ROYAL PSALMS

day *one*

READ

1 Why do the nations rage
    and the peoples plot in vain?
2 The kings of the earth set themselves,
    and the rulers take counsel together,
    against the Lord and against his Anointed, saying,
3 "Let us burst their bonds apart
    and cast away their cords from us."

4 He who sits in the heavens laughs;
    the Lord holds them in derision.
5 Then he will speak to them in his wrath,
    and terrify them in his fury, saying,
6 "As for me, I have set my King
    on Zion, my holy hill."

7 I will tell of the decree:
The Lord said to me, "You are my Son;
    today I have begotten you.
8 Ask of me, and I will make the nations your heritage,
    and the ends of the earth your possession.
9 You shall break them with a rod of iron
    and dash them in pieces like a potter's vessel."

10 Now therefore, O kings, be wise;
    be warned, O rulers of the earth.
11 Serve the Lord with fear,
    and rejoice with trembling.
12 Kiss the Son,
    lest he be angry, and you perish in the way,
    for his wrath is quickly kindled.
Blessed are all who take refuge in him.

OBSERVE	INTERPRET

KEY WORDS	DEFINITIONS	CROSS REFERENCES

MAIN POINT(S)	APPLY

PRAY

day *two*

PSALM 20

READ

¹ May the Lord answer you in the day of trouble!
   May the name of the God of Jacob protect you!
² May he send you help from the sanctuary
   and give you support from Zion!
³ May he remember all your offerings
   and regard with favor your burnt sacrifices!   *Selah*

⁴ May he grant you your heart's desire
   and fulfill all your plans!
⁵ May we shout for joy over your salvation,
   and in the name of our God set up our banners!
May the Lord fulfill all your petitions!

⁶ Now I know that the Lord saves his anointed;
   he will answer him from his holy heaven
   with the saving might of his right hand.
⁷ Some trust in chariots and some in horses,
   but we trust in the name of the Lord our God.
⁸ They collapse and fall,
   but we rise and stand upright.

⁹ O Lord, save the king!
   May he answer us when we call.

OBSERVE	INTERPRET

KEY WORDS	DEFINITIONS	CROSS REFERENCES

MAIN POINT(S)

APPLY

PRAY

day *three*

PSALM 21

READ

[1] O Lord, in your strength the king rejoices,
    and in your salvation how greatly he exults!
[2] You have given him his heart's desire
    and have not withheld the request of his lips.   *Selah*
[3] For you meet him with rich blessings;
    you set a crown of fine gold upon his head.
[4] He asked life of you; you gave it to him,
    length of days forever and ever.
[5] His glory is great through your salvation;
    splendor and majesty you bestow on him.
[6] For you make him most blessed forever;
    you make him glad with the joy of your presence.
[7] For the king trusts in the Lord,
    and through the steadfast love of the Most High he shall not be moved.

[8] Your hand will find out all your enemies;
    your right hand will find out those who hate you.
[9] You will make them as a blazing oven
    when you appear.
The Lord will swallow them up in his wrath,
    and fire will consume them.
[10] You will destroy their descendants from the earth,
    and their offspring from among the children of man.
[11] Though they plan evil against you,
    though they devise mischief, they will not succeed.
[12] For you will put them to flight;
    you will aim at their faces with your bows.

[13] Be exalted, O Lord, in your strength!
    We will sing and praise your power.

OBSERVE	INTERPRET

KEY WORDS	DEFINITIONS	CROSS REFERENCES

MAIN POINT(S)	APPLY

PRAY

day *four*

PSALM 110

READ

¹ The Lord says to my Lord:
  "Sit at my right hand,
until I make your enemies your footstool."

² The Lord sends forth from Zion
  your mighty scepter.
  Rule in the midst of your enemies!
³ Your people will offer themselves freely
  on the day of your power,
  in holy garments;
from the womb of the morning,
  the dew of your youth will be yours.
⁴ The Lord has sworn
  and will not change his mind,
"You are a priest forever
  after the order of Melchizedek."

⁵ The Lord is at your right hand;
  he will shatter kings on the day of his wrath.
⁶ He will execute judgment among the nations,
  filling them with corpses;
he will shatter chiefs
  over the wide earth.
⁷ He will drink from the brook by the way;
  therefore he will lift up his head.

OBSERVE	INTERPRET

KEY WORDS	DEFINITIONS	CROSS REFERENCES

MAIN POINT(S)

APPLY

PRAY

day *five*

ROYAL PSALMS | REVIEW & DISCUSSION QUESTIONS

1 Summarize what you learned from this week's royal psalms.

2 Which psalm or verse was your favorite? Explain.

3 Did you notice any common themes or elements in these royal psalms?

4 In the royal psalms, the king is a central figure. Share an extravagant word picture used to extol the king.

5 In most Ancient Near East nations, a king was seen as divine and enjoyed ultimate authority. Do these psalms present any clues as to whether or not this is true in Israel?

6 Do you notice any special relationships between God and the king?

7 What instruction to the king is meaningful to you?

8 Psalms 2 & 110 glorify the king far above any reality for the monarchs of the Davidic line and point to a true king. Did you notice any aspect of a king that no earthly king could possibly fulfill?

9 Define *anointed* in Psalm 2:2. To whom is this referring?

10 What can we learn about praying for our leaders from these psalms? (See Romans 13:1.)

11 What did you learn about God through these royal psalms?

12 What did you learn about how to worship God?

take it to *heart*

BUT YOU, O LORD,
DO NOT BE FAR OFF!
O YOU MY HELP, COME
QUICKLY TO MY AID!

PSALM 22:19

chapter *three*

LAMENT PSALMS

take *note*

LAMENT PSALMS

take *note*

LAMENT PSALMS

day *one*

PSALM 3

READ

¹ O Lord, how many are my foes!
   Many are rising against me;
² many are saying of my soul,
   "There is no salvation for him in God."   *Selah*

³ But you, O Lord, are a shield about me,
   my glory, and the lifter of my head.
⁴ I cried aloud to the Lord,
   and he answered me from his holy hill.   *Selah*

⁵ I lay down and slept;
   I woke again, for the Lord sustained me.
⁶ I will not be afraid of many thousands of people
   who have set themselves against me all around.

⁷ Arise, O Lord!
   Save me, O my God!
For you strike all my enemies on the cheek;
   you break the teeth of the wicked.

⁸ Salvation belongs to the Lord;
   your blessing be on your people!   *Selah*

OBSERVE	INTERPRET

KEY WORDS	DEFINITIONS	CROSS REFERENCES

MAIN POINT(S)

APPLY

PRAY

day *two*

PSALM 13

READ

¹ How long, O Lord? Will you forget me forever?
    How long will you hide your face from me?
² How long must I take counsel in my soul
    and have sorrow in my heart all the day?
How long shall my enemy be exalted over me?

³ Consider and answer me, O Lord my God;
    light up my eyes, lest I sleep the sleep of death,
⁴ lest my enemy say, "I have prevailed over him,"
    lest my foes rejoice because I am shaken.

⁵ But I have trusted in your steadfast love;
    my heart shall rejoice in your salvation.
⁶ I will sing to the Lord,
    because he has dealt bountifully with me.

OBSERVE	INTERPRET

KEY WORDS	DEFINITIONS	CROSS REFERENCES

MAIN POINT(S)	APPLY

PRAY

day *three*

READ

1 My God, my God, why have you forsaken me?
  Why are you so far from saving me, from the words of my groaning?
2 O my God, I cry by day, but you do not answer,
  and by night, but I find no rest.

3 Yet you are holy,
  enthroned on the praises of Israel.
4 In you our fathers trusted;
  they trusted, and you delivered them.
5 To you they cried and were rescued;
  in you they trusted and were not put to shame.

6 But I am a worm and not a man,
  scorned by mankind and despised by the people.
7 All who see me mock me;
  they make mouths at me; they wag their heads;
8 "He trusts in the Lord; let him deliver him;
  let him rescue him, for he delights in him!"

9 Yet you are he who took me from the womb;
  you made me trust you at my mother's breasts.
10 On you was I cast from my birth,
  and from my mother's womb you have been my God.
11 Be not far from me,
  for trouble is near,
  and there is none to help.

12 Many bulls encompass me;
  strong bulls of Bashan surround me;
13 they open wide their mouths at me,
  like a ravening and roaring lion.

¹⁴ I am poured out like water,
   and all my bones are out of joint;
my heart is like wax;
   it is melted within my breast;
¹⁵ my strength is dried up like a potsherd,
   and my tongue sticks to my jaws;
   you lay me in the dust of death.

¹⁶ For dogs encompass me;
   a company of evildoers encircles me;
they have pierced my hands and feet—
¹⁷ I can count all my bones—
they stare and gloat over me;
¹⁸ they divide my garments among them,
   and for my clothing they cast lots.

¹⁹ But you, O Lord, do not be far off!
   O you my help, come quickly to my aid!
²⁰ Deliver my soul from the sword,
   my precious life from the power of the dog!
²¹   Save me from the mouth of the lion!
You have rescued me from the horns of the wild oxen!

²² I will tell of your name to my brothers;
   in the midst of the congregation I will praise you:
²³ You who fear the Lord, praise him!
   All you offspring of Jacob, glorify him,
   and stand in awe of him, all you offspring of Israel!
²⁴ For he has not despised or abhorred
   the affliction of the afflicted,
and he has not hidden his face from him,
   but has heard, when he cried to him.

²⁵ From you comes my praise in the great congregation;
   my vows I will perform before those who fear him.
²⁶ The afflicted shall eat and be satisfied;
   those who seek him shall praise the Lord!

May your hearts live forever!

27 All the ends of the earth shall remember
   and turn to the Lord,
and all the families of the nations
   shall worship before you.
28 For kingship belongs to the Lord,
   and he rules over the nations.

29 All the prosperous of the earth eat and worship;
   before him shall bow all who go down to the dust,
   even the one who could not keep himself alive.
30 Posterity shall serve him;
   it shall be told of the Lord to the coming generation;
31 they shall come and proclaim his righteousness to a people yet unborn,
   that he has done it.

OBSERVE	INTERPRET

KEY WORDS	DEFINITIONS	CROSS REFERENCES

MAIN POINT(S)	APPLY

PRAY

day *four*

PSALM 20

READ

1 Be merciful to me, O God, be merciful to me,
  for in you my soul takes refuge;
in the shadow of your wings I will take refuge,
  till the storms of destruction pass by.
2 I cry out to God Most High,
  to God who fulfills his purpose for me.
3 He will send from heaven and save me;
  he will put to shame him who tramples on me.   *Selah*
God will send out his steadfast love and his faithfulness!

4 My soul is in the midst of lions;
  I lie down amid fiery beasts—
the children of man, whose teeth are spears and arrows,
  whose tongues are sharp swords.

5 Be exalted, O God, above the heavens!
  Let your glory be over all the earth!

6 They set a net for my steps;
  my soul was bowed down.
They dug a pit in my way,
  but they have fallen into it themselves.   *Selah*
7 My heart is steadfast, O God,
  my heart is steadfast!
I will sing and make melody!
8   Awake, my glory!
Awake, O harp and lyre!
  I will awake the dawn!
9 I will give thanks to you, O Lord, among the peoples;
  I will sing praises to you among the nations.
10 For your steadfast love is great to the heavens,
  your faithfulness to the clouds.

11 Be exalted, O God, above the heavens!
  Let your glory be over all the earth!

OBSERVE	INTERPRET

KEY WORDS	DEFINITIONS	CROSS REFERENCES

MAIN POINT(S)

APPLY

PRAY

day *five*

LAMENT PSALMS | REVIEW & DISCUSSION QUESTIONS

1 Summarize what you learned from this week's lament psalms.	2 Which psalm or verse was your favorite? Explain.
3 Did you notice any common themes or elements in these lament psalms?	4 Of the four psalms, which *address* or *cry to God* gained your attention?
5 Did you relate to a particular complaint? Please share.	6 Provide an example of the psalmist's expression of trust in God.

7 Please share a relatable *petition* (plea for help) from one of these psalms.

8 Most lament psalms also include a vow of praise and thanksgiving. Highlight one that is meaningful to you.

9 How would you describe the difference between whining to God and lamenting to God?

10 Do these psalms stir up an honest cry, plea, or question in your own heart to ask God?

11 What did you learn about God through these lament psalms?

12 What did you discover about how to worship God in times of grief, sorrow, anger, or shame?

take it to *heart*

USE THIS SPACE TO WRITE OUT OR JOURNAL A FAVORITE VERSE FROM THIS WEEK'S STUDY, OR WRITE OUT YOUR OWN LAMENT PSALM. (THIS IS BETWEEN YOU AND GOD.)

I WAITED PATIENTLY
FOR THE LORD;
HE INCLINED TO ME
AND HEARD MY CRY.

PSALM 40:1

chapter *four*

LAMENT PSALMS

take *note*

LAMENT PSALMS

take *note*

LAMENT PSALMS

day *one*

> READ
>
> ¹ I said, "I will guard my ways,
>   that I may not sin with my tongue;
> I will guard my mouth with a muzzle,
>   so long as the wicked are in my presence."
> ² I was mute and silent;
>   I held my peace to no avail,
> and my distress grew worse.
> ³   My heart became hot within me.
> As I mused, the fire burned;
>   then I spoke with my tongue:
>
> ⁴ "O Lord, make me know my end
>   and what is the measure of my days;
>   let me know how fleeting I am!
> ⁵ Behold, you have made my days a few handbreadths,
>   and my lifetime is as nothing before you.
> Surely all mankind stands as a mere breath! Selah
> ⁶   Surely a man goes about as a shadow!
> Surely for nothing they are in turmoil;
>   man heaps up wealth and does not know who will gather!
>
> ⁷ "And now, O Lord, for what do I wait?
>   My hope is in you.
> ⁸ Deliver me from all my transgressions.
>   Do not make me the scorn of the fool!
> ⁹ I am mute; I do not open my mouth,
>   for it is you who have done it.
> ¹⁰ Remove your stroke from me;
>   I am spent by the hostility of your hand.

¹¹ When you discipline a man
  with rebukes for sin,
you consume like a moth what is dear to him;
  surely all mankind is a mere breath! Selah

¹² "Hear my prayer, O Lord,
  and give ear to my cry;
  hold not your peace at my tears!
For I am a sojourner with you,
  a guest, like all my fathers.
¹³ Look away from me, that I may smile again,
  before I depart and am no more!"

OBSERVE	INTERPRET

KEY WORDS	DEFINITIONS	CROSS REFERENCES

MAIN POINT(S)

APPLY

PRAY

day *two*

PSALM 40

READ

¹ I waited patiently for the Lord;
   he inclined to me and heard my cry.
² He drew me up from the pit of destruction,
   out of the miry bog,
and set my feet upon a rock,
   making my steps secure.
³ He put a new song in my mouth,
   a song of praise to our God.
Many will see and fear,
   and put their trust in the Lord.

⁴ Blessed is the man who makes
   the Lord his trust,
who does not turn to the proud,
   to those who go astray after a lie!
⁵ You have multiplied, O Lord my God,
   your wondrous deeds and your thoughts toward us;
   none can compare with you!
I will proclaim and tell of them,
   yet they are more than can be told.

⁶ In sacrifice and offering you have not delighted,
   but you have given me an open ear.
Burnt offering and sin offering
   you have not required.
⁷ Then I said, "Behold, I have come;
   in the scroll of the book it is written of me:
⁸ I delight to do your will, O my God;
   your law is within my heart."

⁹ I have told the glad news of deliverance
   in the great congregation;
behold, I have not restrained my lips,
   as you know, O Lord.
¹⁰ I have not hidden your deliverance within my heart;
   I have spoken of your faithfulness and your salvation;
I have not concealed your steadfast love and your faithfulness
   from the great congregation.

¹¹ As for you, O Lord, you will not restrain
   your mercy from me;
your steadfast love and your faithfulness will
   ever preserve me!
¹² For evils have encompassed me
   beyond number;
my iniquities have overtaken me,
   and I cannot see;
they are more than the hairs of my head;
   my heart fails me.

¹³ Be pleased, O Lord, to deliver me!
   O Lord, make haste to help me!
¹⁴ Let those be put to shame and disappointed altogether
   who seek to snatch away my life;
let those be turned back and brought to dishonor
   who delight in my hurt!
¹⁵ Let those be appalled because of their shame
   who say to me, "Aha, Aha!"

¹⁶ But may all who seek you
   rejoice and be glad in you;
may those who love your salvation
   say continually, "Great is the Lord!"
¹⁷ As for me, I am poor and needy,
   but the Lord takes thought for me.
You are my help and my deliverer;
   do not delay, O my God!

OBSERVE	INTERPRET

KEY WORDS	DEFINITIONS	CROSS REFERENCES

MAIN POINT(S)	APPLY

PRAY

day *three*

PSALM 42

READ

[1] As a deer pants for flowing streams,
    so pants my soul for you, O God.
[2] My soul thirsts for God,
    for the living God.
When shall I come and appear before God?
[3] My tears have been my food
    day and night,
while they say to me all the day long,
    "Where is your God?"
[4] These things I remember,
    as I pour out my soul:
how I would go with the throng
    and lead them in procession to the house of God
with glad shouts and songs of praise,
    a multitude keeping festival.

[5] Why are you cast down, O my soul,
    and why are you in turmoil within me?
Hope in God; for I shall again praise him,
    my salvation [6] and my God.

My soul is cast down within me;
    therefore I remember you
from the land of Jordan and of Hermon,
    from Mount Mizar.
[7] Deep calls to deep
    at the roar of your waterfalls;
all your breakers and your waves
    have gone over me.

⁸ By day the Lord commands his steadfast love,
 and at night his song is with me,
 a prayer to the God of my life.
⁹ I say to God, my rock:
 "Why have you forgotten me?
Why do I go mourning
 because of the oppression of the enemy?"
¹⁰ As with a deadly wound in my bones,
 my adversaries taunt me,
while they say to me all the day long,
 "Where is your God?"

¹¹ Why are you cast down, O my soul,
 and why are you in turmoil within me?
Hope in God; for I shall again praise him,
 my salvation and my God.

OBSERVE	INTERPRET

KEY WORDS	DEFINITIONS	CROSS REFERENCES

MAIN POINT(S)

APPLY

PRAY

FOR YOU ARE THE GOD
IN WHOM I TAKE REFUGE...

PSALM 43:2

day *four*

READ

¹ Vindicate me, O God, and defend my cause
    against an ungodly people,
from the deceitful and unjust man
    deliver me!
² For you are the God in whom I take refuge;
    why have you rejected me?
Why do I go about mourning
    because of the oppression of the enemy?

³ Send out your light and your truth;
    let them lead me;
let them bring me to your holy hill
    and to your dwelling!
⁴ Then I will go to the altar of God,
    to God my exceeding joy,
and I will praise you with the lyre,
    O God, my God.

⁵ Why are you cast down, O my soul,
    and why are you in turmoil within me?
Hope in God; for I shall again praise him,
    my salvation and my God.

OBSERVE	INTERPRET

KEY WORDS	DEFINITIONS	CROSS REFERENCES

MAIN POINT(S)	APPLY

PRAY

day *five*

1 Summarize what you learned from this week's lament psalms.	2 Which psalm or verse was your favorite? Explain.
3 Did you notice any common themes or elements in these lament psalms?	4 Of the four psalms, which *address* or *cry to God* gained your attention?
5 Did you relate to a particular complaint? Please share.	6 Provide an example of the psalmist's expression of trust in God.

7 Please share a relatable *petition* (plea for help) from one of these psalms.

8 Lament psalms include a vow of praise and thanksgiving. Highlight one that is meaningful to you.

9 "In this world we have trouble." (John 16:33) Practically, what do you learn from psalmist about working through a crisis with God?

10 How do we learn to praise and thank God in the midst of trials?

11 What did you learn about God through these lament psalms? (See Philippians 4:4-8.)

12 What else have you discovered about how to worship God in times of grief, sorrow, anger, or shame?

take it to *heart*

SHOW US YOUR STEADFAST
LOVE, O LORD, AND GRANT
US YOUR SALVATION.

PSALM 85:7

chapter *five*

COMMUNAL LAMENT PSALMS

take *note*

COMMUNAL LAMENT PSALMS

take *note*

COMMUNAL LAMENT PSALMS

day *one*

READ

¹ Give ear, O Shepherd of Israel,
   you who lead Joseph like a flock.
You who are enthroned upon the cherubim, shine forth.
²   Before Ephraim and Benjamin and Manasseh,
stir up your might
   and come to save us!

³ Restore us, O God;
   let your face shine, that we may be saved!

⁴ O Lord God of hosts,
   how long will you be angry with your people's prayers?
⁵ You have fed them with the bread of tears
   and given them tears to drink in full measure.
⁶ You make us an object of contention for our neighbors,
   and our enemies laugh among themselves.

⁷ Restore us, O God of hosts;
   let your face shine, that we may be saved!

⁸ You brought a vine out of Egypt;
   you drove out the nations and planted it.
⁹ You cleared the ground for it;
   it took deep root and filled the land.
¹⁰ The mountains were covered with its shade,
   the mighty cedars with its branches.
¹¹ It sent out its branches to the sea
   and its shoots to the River.
¹² Why then have you broken down its walls,
   so that all who pass along the way pluck its fruit?

---

¹³ The boar from the forest ravages it,
and all that move in the field feed on it.

¹⁴ Turn again, O God of hosts!
Look down from heaven, and see;
have regard for this vine,
¹⁵   the stock that your right hand planted,
and for the son whom you made strong for yourself.
¹⁶ They have burned it with fire; they have cut it down;
may they perish at the rebuke of your face!
¹⁷ But let your hand be on the man of your right hand,
the son of man whom you have made strong for yourself!
¹⁸ Then we shall not turn back from you;
give us life, and we will call upon your name!

¹⁹ Restore us, O Lord God of hosts!
Let your face shine, that we may be saved!

OBSERVE	INTERPRET

KEY WORDS	DEFINITIONS	CROSS REFERENCES

MAIN POINT(S)	APPLY

PRAY

day *two*

PSALM 85

READ

¹ Lord, you were favorable to your land;
   you restored the fortunes of Jacob.
² You forgave the iniquity of your people;
   you covered all their sin. Selah
³ You withdrew all your wrath;
   you turned from your hot anger.

⁴ Restore us again, O God of our salvation,
   and put away your indignation toward us!
⁵ Will you be angry with us forever?
   Will you prolong your anger to all generations?
⁶ Will you not revive us again,
   that your people may rejoice in you?
⁷ Show us your steadfast love, O Lord,
   and grant us your salvation.

⁸ Let me hear what God the Lord will speak,
   for he will speak peace to his people, to his saints;
   but let them not turn back to folly.
⁹ Surely his salvation is near to those who fear him,
   that glory may dwell in our land.

¹⁰ Steadfast love and faithfulness meet;
   righteousness and peace kiss each other.
¹¹ Faithfulness springs up from the ground,
   and righteousness looks down from the sky.
¹² Yes, the Lord will give what is good,
   and our land will yield its increase.
¹³ Righteousness will go before him
   and make his footsteps a way.

OBSERVE	INTERPRET

KEY WORDS	DEFINITIONS	CROSS REFERENCES

MAIN POINT(S)

APPLY

PRAY

day *three*

READ

¹ Lord, you have been our dwelling place
    in all generations.
² Before the mountains were brought forth,
    or ever you had formed the earth and the world,
    from everlasting to everlasting you are God.

³ You return man to dust
    and say, "Return, O children of man!"
⁴ For a thousand years in your sight
    are but as yesterday when it is past,
    or as a watch in the night.

⁵ You sweep them away as with a flood; they are like a dream,
    like grass that is renewed in the morning:
⁶ in the morning it flourishes and is renewed;
    in the evening it fades and withers.

⁷ For we are brought to an end by your anger;
    by your wrath we are dismayed.
⁸ You have set our iniquities before you,
    our secret sins in the light of your presence.

⁹ For all our days pass away under your wrath;
    we bring our years to an end like a sigh.
¹⁰ The years of our life are seventy,
    or even by reason of strength eighty;
yet their span is but toil and trouble;
    they are soon gone, and we fly away.
¹¹ Who considers the power of your anger,
    and your wrath according to the fear of you?

¹² So teach us to number our days
  that we may get a heart of wisdom.
¹³ Return, O Lord! How long?
  Have pity on your servants!
¹⁴ Satisfy us in the morning with your steadfast love,
  that we may rejoice and be glad all our days.
¹⁵ Make us glad for as many days as you have afflicted us,
  and for as many years as we have seen evil.
¹⁶ Let your work be shown to your servants,
  and your glorious power to their children.
¹⁷ Let the favor of the Lord our God be upon us,
  and establish the work of our hands upon us;
  yes, establish the work of our hands!

OBSERVE	INTERPRET

KEY WORDS	DEFINITIONS	CROSS REFERENCES

MAIN POINT(S)	APPLY

PRAY

day *four*

PSALM 137

READ

¹ By the waters of Babylon,
    there we sat down and wept,
    when we remembered Zion.
² On the willows there
    we hung up our lyres.
³ For there our captors
    required of us songs,
and our tormentors, mirth, saying,
    "Sing us one of the songs of Zion!"

⁴ How shall we sing the Lord's song
    in a foreign land?
⁵ If I forget you, O Jerusalem,
    let my right hand forget its skill!
⁶ Let my tongue stick to the roof of my mouth,
    if I do not remember you,
if I do not set Jerusalem
    above my highest joy!

⁷ Remember, O Lord, against the Edomites
    the day of Jerusalem,
how they said, "Lay it bare, lay it bare,
    down to its foundations!"
⁸ O daughter of Babylon, doomed to be destroyed,
    blessed shall he be who repays you
    with what you have done to us!
⁹ Blessed shall he be who takes your little ones
    and dashes them against the rock!

OBSERVE

INTERPRET

KEY WORDS	DEFINITIONS	CROSS REFERENCES

MAIN POINT(S)	APPLY

PRAY

day *five*

1 Summarize what you learned from these communal lament psalms.

2 Which psalm or verse was your favorite? Explain.

3 Did you notice any common themes or elements in these psalms?

4 Of this week's psalms, which *address* or *cry to God* gained your attention?

5 Did you relate to a particular complaint? Please share.

6 Provide an example of a psalmist's expression of trust in God.

7 Please share a relatable *petition* (plea for help) from one of these psalms.

8 Highlight a vow of praise and thanksgiving that is meaningful to you.

9 Sometimes a psalmist uses very vivid and exaggerated imagery to express raw emotion. (137:8-9) How do you explain this?

10 We tend to live individualistically. What do these communal lament psalms teach us about praying for our church family? What burdens are on your heart for your community?

11 What did you learn about God through these lament psalms?

12 What did you discover about how to worship God communally in times of grief, sorrow, anger, or shame?

take it to *heart*

USE THIS SPACE TO WRITE OUT OR JOURNAL A FAVORITE VERSE FROM THIS WEEK'S STUDY, OR WRITE OUT YOUR OWN COMMUNAL LAMENT PSALM. (THIS IS BETWEEN YOU AND GOD.)

I SAID, "I WILL CONFESS MY
TRANSGRESSIONS TO THE
LORD," AND YOU FORGAVE
THE INIQUITY OF MY SIN.

PSALM 32:5

chapter *six*

PENITENTIAL PSALMS

take *note*

PENITENTIAL PSALMS

take *note*

PENITENTIAL PSALMS

day *one*

READ

¹ Blessed is the one whose transgression is forgiven,
  whose sin is covered.
² Blessed is the man against whom the Lord counts no iniquity,
  and in whose spirit there is no deceit.

³ For when I kept silent, my bones wasted away
  through my groaning all day long.
⁴ For day and night your hand was heavy upon me;
  my strength was dried up as by the heat of summer.   *Selah*

⁵ I acknowledged my sin to you,
  and I did not cover my iniquity;
I said, "I will confess my transgressions to the Lord,"
  and you forgave the iniquity of my sin.   *Selah*

⁶ Therefore let everyone who is godly
  offer prayer to you at a time when you may be found;
surely in the rush of great waters,
  they shall not reach him.
⁷ You are a hiding place for me;
  you preserve me from trouble;
  you surround me with shouts of deliverance.   *Selah*

⁸ I will instruct you and teach you in the way you should go;
  I will counsel you with my eye upon you.
⁹ Be not like a horse or a mule, without understanding,
  which must be curbed with bit and bridle,
  or it will not stay near you.

¹⁰ Many are the sorrows of the wicked,
   but steadfast love surrounds the one who trusts in the Lord.
¹¹ Be glad in the Lord, and rejoice, O righteous,
   and shout for joy, all you upright in heart!

OBSERVE	INTERPRET

KEY WORDS	DEFINITIONS	CROSS REFERENCES

MAIN POINT(S)

APPLY

PRAY

day *two*

READ

¹ Have mercy on me, O God,
 according to your steadfast love;
according to your abundant mercy
 blot out my transgressions.
² Wash me thoroughly from my iniquity,
 and cleanse me from my sin!

³ For I know my transgressions,
 and my sin is ever before me.
⁴ Against you, you only, have I sinned
 and done what is evil in your sight,
so that you may be justified in your words
 and blameless in your judgment.
⁵ Behold, I was brought forth in iniquity,
 and in sin did my mother conceive me.
⁶ Behold, you delight in truth in the inward being,
 and you teach me wisdom in the secret heart.

⁷ Purge me with hyssop, and I shall be clean;
 wash me, and I shall be whiter than snow.
⁸ Let me hear joy and gladness;
 let the bones that you have broken rejoice.
⁹ Hide your face from my sins,
 and blot out all my iniquities.
¹⁰ Create in me a clean heart, O God,
 and renew a right spirit within me.
¹¹ Cast me not away from your presence,
 and take not your Holy Spirit from me.
¹² Restore to me the joy of your salvation,
 and uphold me with a willing spirit.

¹³ Then I will teach transgressors your ways,
   and sinners will return to you.
¹⁴ Deliver me from bloodguiltiness, O God,
   O God of my salvation,
   and my tongue will sing aloud of your righteousness.
¹⁵ O Lord, open my lips,
   and my mouth will declare your praise.
¹⁶ For you will not delight in sacrifice, or I would give it;
   you will not be pleased with a burnt offering.
¹⁷ The sacrifices of God are a broken spirit;
   a broken and contrite heart, O God, you will not despise.

¹⁸ Do good to Zion in your good pleasure;
   build up the walls of Jerusalem;
¹⁹ then will you delight in right sacrifices,
   in burnt offerings and whole burnt offerings;
   then bulls will be offered on your altar.

OBSERVE	INTERPRET

KEY WORDS	DEFINITIONS	CROSS REFERENCES

MAIN POINT(S)	APPLY

PRAY

day *three*

PSALM 139

READ

¹ O Lord, you have searched me and known me!
² You know when I sit down and when I rise up;
   you discern my thoughts from afar.
³ You search out my path and my lying down
   and are acquainted with all my ways.
⁴ Even before a word is on my tongue,
   behold, O Lord, you know it altogether.
⁵ You hem me in, behind and before,
   and lay your hand upon me.
⁶ Such knowledge is too wonderful for me;
   it is high; I cannot attain it.

⁷ Where shall I go from your Spirit?
   Or where shall I flee from your presence?
⁸ If I ascend to heaven, you are there!
   If I make my bed in Sheol, you are there!
⁹ If I take the wings of the morning
   and dwell in the uttermost parts of the sea,
¹⁰ even there your hand shall lead me,
   and your right hand shall hold me.
¹¹ If I say, "Surely the darkness shall cover me,
   and the light about me be night,"
¹² even the darkness is not dark to you;
   the night is bright as the day,
   for darkness is as light with you.

¹³ For you formed my inward parts;
   you knitted me together in my mother's womb.
¹⁴ I praise you, for I am fearfully and wonderfully made.
Wonderful are your works;
   my soul knows it very well.

---

¹⁵ My frame was not hidden from you,
when I was being made in secret,
    intricately woven in the depths of the earth.
¹⁶ Your eyes saw my unformed substance;
in your book were written, every one of them,
    the days that were formed for me,
    when as yet there was none of them.

¹⁷ How precious to me are your thoughts, O God!
    How vast is the sum of them!
¹⁸ If I would count them, they are more than the sand.
    I awake, and I am still with you.

¹⁹ Oh that you would slay the wicked, O God!
    O men of blood, depart from me!
²⁰ They speak against you with malicious intent;
    your enemies take your name in vain.
²¹ Do I not hate those who hate you, O Lord?
    And do I not loathe those who rise up against you?
²² I hate them with complete hatred;
    I count them my enemies.

²³ Search me, O God, and know my heart!
    Try me and know my thoughts!
⁻ And see if there be any grievous way in me,
    and lead me in the way everlasting!

OBSERVE	INTERPRET

KEY WORDS	DEFINITIONS	CROSS REFERENCES

MAIN POINT(S)	APPLY

PRAY

day *four*

PSALM 143

READ

¹ Hear my prayer, O Lord;
   give ear to my pleas for mercy!
   In your faithfulness answer me, in your righteousness!
² Enter not into judgment with your servant,
   for no one living is righteous before you.

³ For the enemy has pursued my soul;
   he has crushed my life to the ground;
   he has made me sit in darkness like those long dead.
⁴ Therefore my spirit faints within me;
   my heart within me is appalled.

⁵ I remember the days of old;
   I meditate on all that you have done;
   I ponder the work of your hands.
⁶ I stretch out my hands to you;
   my soul thirsts for you like a parched land. Selah

⁷ Answer me quickly, O Lord!
   My spirit fails!
Hide not your face from me,
   lest I be like those who go down to the pit.
⁸ Let me hear in the morning of your steadfast love,
   for in you I trust.
Make me know the way I should go,
   for to you I lift up my soul.

⁹ Deliver me from my enemies, O Lord!
    I have fled to you for refuge.
¹⁰ Teach me to do your will,
    for you are my God!
Let your good Spirit lead me
    on level ground!

¹¹ For your name's sake, O Lord, preserve my life!
    In your righteousness bring my soul out of trouble!
¹² And in your steadfast love you will cut off my enemies,
    and you will destroy all the adversaries of my soul,
    for I am your servant.

OBSERVE	INTERPRET

KEY WORDS	DEFINITIONS	CROSS REFERENCES

MAIN POINT(S)

APPLY

PRAY

day *five*

1 Summarize what you learned from this week's penitential psalms.

2 Which psalm or verse was your favorite? Explain.

3 Did you notice any common themes or elements in these psalms?

4 Penitential psalms usually include a confession of sin. Did a particular confession glean your attention?

5 What is the purpose of confession? (See I John 1:9, James 5:16, and I Peter 5:6.)

6 Define *sin*.

7 According to Psalm 51:1 and 143:1, what is the only basis for approaching God in our sin? Practically, what does working through guilt with God look like?

8 How is Psalm 32 different from the other penitential psalms?

9 Provide an example of a psalmist's expression of trust in God.

10 Please share a relatable petition (plea for help) from one of these psalms.

11 What did these penitential psalms teach you about God Himself?

12 What did you discover about worshipping God in times of remorse or regret?

take it to *heart*

USE THIS SPACE TO WRITE OUT OR JOURNAL A FAVORITE VERSE FROM THIS WEEK'S STUDY, OR WRITE OUT YOUR OWN PENITENTIAL PSALM. (THIS IS BETWEEN YOU AND GOD.)

I WILL SAY TO THE LORD,
"MY REFUGE AND MY FORTRESS,
MY GOD, IN WHOM I TRUST."

PSALM 91:2

chapter *seven*

TRUST PSALMS

take *note*

TRUST PSALMS

take *note*

TRUST PSALMS

day *one*

PSALM 23

READ

¹ The Lord is my shepherd; I shall not want.
²   He makes me lie down in green pastures.
He leads me beside still waters.
³   He restores my soul.
He leads me in paths of righteousness
    for his name's sake.

⁴ Even though I walk through the valley of the shadow of death,
    I will fear no evil,
for you are with me;
    your rod and your staff,
    they comfort me.

⁵ You prepare a table before me
    in the presence of my enemies;
you anoint my head with oil;
    my cup overflows.
⁶ Surely goodness and mercy shall follow me
    all the days of my life,
and I shall dwell in the house of the Lord
    forever.

OBSERVE	INTERPRET

KEY WORDS	DEFINITIONS	CROSS REFERENCES

MAIN POINT(S)	APPLY

PRAY

day *two*

PSALM 63

READ

[1] O God, you are my God; earnestly I seek you;
   my soul thirsts for you;
my flesh faints for you,
   as in a dry and weary land where there is no water.
[2] So I have looked upon you in the sanctuary,
   beholding your power and glory.
[3] Because your steadfast love is better than life,
   my lips will praise you.
[4] So I will bless you as long as I live;
   in your name I will lift up my hands.

[5] My soul will be satisfied as with fat and rich food,
   and my mouth will praise you with joyful lips,
[6] when I remember you upon my bed,
   and meditate on you in the watches of the night;
[7] for you have been my help,
   and in the shadow of your wings I will sing for joy.
[8] My soul clings to you;
   your right hand upholds me.

[9] But those who seek to destroy my life
   shall go down into the depths of the earth;
[10] they shall be given over to the power of the sword;
   they shall be a portion for jackals.
[11] But the king shall rejoice in God;
   all who swear by him shall exult,
      for the mouths of liars will be stopped.

OBSERVE	INTERPRET

KEY WORDS	DEFINITIONS	CROSS REFERENCES

MAIN POINT(S)

APPLY

PRAY

day *three*

PSALM 91

READ

¹ He who dwells in the shelter of the Most High
    will abide in the shadow of the Almighty.
² I will say to the Lord, "My refuge and my fortress,
    my God, in whom I trust."

³ For he will deliver you from the snare of the fowler
    and from the deadly pestilence.
⁴ He will cover you with his pinions,
    and under his wings you will find refuge;
    his faithfulness is a shield and buckler.
⁵ You will not fear the terror of the night,
    nor the arrow that flies by day,
⁶ nor the pestilence that stalks in darkness,
    nor the destruction that wastes at noonday.

⁷ A thousand may fall at your side,
    ten thousand at your right hand,
    but it will not come near you.
⁸ You will only look with your eyes
    and see the recompense of the wicked.

⁹ Because you have made the Lord your dwelling place—
    the Most High, who is my refuge—
¹⁰ no evil shall be allowed to befall you,
    no plague come near your tent.

¹¹ For he will command his angels concerning you
    to guard you in all your ways.
¹² On their hands they will bear you up,
    lest you strike your foot against a stone.

¹³ You will tread on the lion and the adder;
   the young lion and the serpent you will trample underfoot.

¹⁴ "Because he holds fast to me in love, I will deliver him;
   I will protect him, because he knows my name.
¹⁵ When he calls to me, I will answer him;
   I will be with him in trouble;
   I will rescue him and honor him.
¹⁶ With long life I will satisfy him
   and show him my salvation."

OBSERVE	INTERPRET

KEY WORDS	DEFINITIONS	CROSS REFERENCES

MAIN POINT(S)	APPLY

PRAY

MY HELP COMES FROM
THE LORD, WHO MADE
HEAVEN AND EARTH.

PSALM 121:2

day *four*

PSALM 121

READ

¹ I lift up my eyes to the hills.
   From where does my help come?
² My help comes from the Lord,
   who made heaven and earth.

³ He will not let your foot be moved;
   he who keeps you will not slumber.
⁴ Behold, he who keeps Israel
   will neither slumber nor sleep.

⁵ The Lord is your keeper;
   the Lord is your shade on your right hand.
⁶ The sun shall not strike you by day,
   nor the moon by night.

⁷ The Lord will keep you from all evil;
   he will keep your life.
⁸ The Lord will keep
   your going out and your coming in
   from this time forth and forevermore.

OBSERVE	INTERPRET

KEY WORDS	DEFINITIONS	CROSS REFERENCES

MAIN POINT(S)

APPLY

PRAY

day *five*

TRUST PSALMS | REVIEW & DISCUSSION QUESTIONS

1 Summarize what you learned from this week's trust psalms.	2 Which psalm or verse was your favorite? Explain.
3 Did you notice any common themes or elements in these psalms?	4 Provide an example of a psalmist's expression of trust in God.
5 Some trust psalms describe how God supplies help in times of need. Please share a meaningful example from one of the psalms.	6 Remember and note a time when God supplied the help you needed.

7 Record a current and specific need you have for God's help and provision. Pray over it using a prayer of trust.

8 A number of trust psalms highlight the nearness of God. Provide a meaningful example from one of this week's psalms.

9 Do you feel near or far from God today? Please explain.

10 What are practical ways to grow in our confidence of the Lord? Share and discuss with others.

11 What did you learn about God through these trust psalms?

12 What did you discover about how to worship God this week?

take it to *heart*

USE THIS SPACE TO WRITE OUT OR JOURNAL A FAVORITE VERSE FROM THIS WEEK'S STUDY, OR WRITE OUT YOUR OWN TRUST PSALM. (THIS IS BETWEEN YOU AND GOD.)

O ISRAEL, HOPE IN THE LORD
FROM THIS TIME FORTH
AND FOREVERMORE.

PSALM 131:3

chapter *eight*

PILGRIM PSALMS

take *note*

PILGRIM PSALMS

take *note*

PILGRIM PSALMS

day *one*

READ

¹ When the Lord restored the fortunes of Zion,
    we were like those who dream.
² Then our mouth was filled with laughter,
    and our tongue with shouts of joy;
then they said among the nations,
    "The Lord has done great things for them."
³ The Lord has done great things for us;
    we are glad.

⁴ Restore our fortunes, O Lord,
    like streams in the Negeb!
⁵ Those who sow in tears
    shall reap with shouts of joy!
⁶ He who goes out weeping,
    bearing the seed for sowing,
shall come home with shouts of joy,
    bringing his sheaves with him.

OBSERVE

INTERPRET

KEY WORDS	DEFINITIONS	CROSS REFERENCES

MAIN POINT(S)	APPLY

PRAY

day *two*

PSALM 127

READ

¹ Unless the Lord builds the house,
    those who build it labor in vain.
Unless the Lord watches over the city,
    the watchman stays awake in vain.
² It is in vain that you rise up early
    and go late to rest,
eating the bread of anxious toil;
    for he gives to his beloved sleep.

³ Behold, children are a heritage from the Lord,
    the fruit of the womb a reward.
⁴ Like arrows in the hand of a warrior
    are the children of one's youth.
⁵ Blessed is the man
    who fills his quiver with them!
He shall not be put to shame
    when he speaks with his enemies in the gate.

OBSERVE	INTERPRET

KEY WORDS	DEFINITIONS	CROSS REFERENCES

MAIN POINT(S)	APPLY

PRAY

day *three*

PSALM 131

READ

[1] O Lord, my heart is not lifted up;
   my eyes are not raised too high;
I do not occupy myself with things
   too great and too marvelous for me.
[2] But I have calmed and quieted my soul,
   like a weaned child with its mother;
   like a weaned child is my soul within me.

[3] O Israel, hope in the Lord
   from this time forth and forevermore.

OBSERVE	INTERPRET

KEY WORDS	DEFINITIONS	CROSS REFERENCES

MAIN POINT(S)

APPLY

PRAY

day *four*

PSALM 133

READ

¹ Behold, how good and pleasant it is
   when brothers dwell in unity!
² It is like the precious oil on the head,
   running down on the beard,
on the beard of Aaron,
   running down on the collar of his robes!
³ It is like the dew of Hermon,
   which falls on the mountains of Zion!
For there the Lord has commanded the blessing,
   life forevermore.

OBSERVE	INTERPRET

KEY WORDS	DEFINITIONS	CROSS REFERENCES

MAIN POINT(S)	APPLY

PRAY

day *five*

1 Summarize what you learned from this week's pilgrim psalms.	2 Which psalm or verse was your favorite? Explain.
3 Did you notice any common themes or elements in these psalms?	4 Which imagery or word picture touched your heart this week?
5 Provide an example of a psalmist's expression of trust in God.	6 Provide a touching example of how God supplied or will supply help in a time of need.

7 Remember that wisdom represented "skill in living." In light of this, what favorite instruction did you find this week?

8 A pilgrim would have looked "up" toward Jerusalem with eyes fixed on the temple. Note a tender expression of joy or rejoicing to worship God.

9 Define *joy*, according to these songs.

10 Jesus taught that "true worshippers will worship God in spirit and truth" (John 4:23-24). In lieu of climbing to Jerusalem, what are practical ways to prepare our hearts for worship?

11 What did you learn about God through these pilgrim psalms?

12 What did you discover about how to worship God this week?

take it to *heart*

USE THIS SPACE TO WRITE OUT OR JOURNAL A FAVORITE VERSE FROM THIS WEEK'S STUDY, OR WRITE OUT YOUR OWN PILGRIM PSALM. (THIS IS BETWEEN YOU AND GOD.)

THE LORD IS ON MY SIDE;
I WILL NOT FEAR.
WHAT CAN MAN DO TO ME?

PSALM 118:6

chapter *nine*

take *note*

THANKSGIVING PSALMS

take *note*

THANKSGIVING PSALMS

day *one*

PSALM 34

READ

1 I will bless the Lord at all times;
   his praise shall continually be in my mouth.
2 My soul makes its boast in the Lord;
   let the humble hear and be glad.
3 Oh, magnify the Lord with me,
   and let us exalt his name together!

4 I sought the Lord, and he answered me
   and delivered me from all my fears.
5 Those who look to him are radiant,
   and their faces shall never be ashamed.
6 This poor man cried, and the Lord heard him
   and saved him out of all his troubles.
7 The angel of the Lord encamps
   around those who fear him, and delivers them.

8 Oh, taste and see that the Lord is good!
   Blessed is the man who takes refuge in him!
9 Oh, fear the Lord, you his saints,
   for those who fear him have no lack!
10 The young lions suffer want and hunger;
   but those who seek the Lord lack no good thing.

11 Come, O children, listen to me;
   I will teach you the fear of the Lord.
12 What man is there who desires life
   and loves many days, that he may see good?
13 Keep your tongue from evil
   and your lips from speaking deceit.

---

¹⁴ Turn away from evil and do good;
　　seek peace and pursue it.

¹⁵ The eyes of the Lord are toward the righteous
　　and his ears toward their cry.
¹⁶ The face of the Lord is against those who do evil,
　　to cut off the memory of them from the earth.
¹⁷ When the righteous cry for help, the Lord hears
　　and delivers them out of all their troubles.
¹⁸ The Lord is near to the brokenhearted
　　and saves the crushed in spirit.

¹⁹ Many are the afflictions of the righteous,
　　but the Lord delivers him out of them all.
²⁰ He keeps all his bones;
　　not one of them is broken.
²¹ Affliction will slay the wicked,
　　and those who hate the righteous will be condemned.
²² The Lord redeems the life of his servants;
　　none of those who take refuge in him will be condemned.

OBSERVE	INTERPRET

KEY WORDS	DEFINITIONS	CROSS REFERENCES

MAIN POINT(S)

APPLY

PRAY

day *two*

PSALM 116

READ

[1] I love the Lord, because he has heard
   my voice and my pleas for mercy.
[2] Because he inclined his ear to me,
   therefore I will call on him as long as I live.
[3] The snares of death encompassed me;
   the pangs of Sheol laid hold on me;
   I suffered distress and anguish.
[4] Then I called on the name of the Lord:
   "O Lord, I pray, deliver my soul!"

[5] Gracious is the Lord, and righteous;
   our God is merciful.
[6] The Lord preserves the simple;
   when I was brought low, he saved me.
[7] Return, O my soul, to your rest;
   for the Lord has dealt bountifully with you.

[8] For you have delivered my soul from death,
   my eyes from tears,
   my feet from stumbling;
[9] I will walk before the Lord
   in the land of the living.

[10] I believed, even when I spoke:
   "I am greatly afflicted";
[11] I said in my alarm,
   "All mankind are liars."

¹² What shall I render to the Lord
   for all his benefits to me?
¹³ I will lift up the cup of salvation
   and call on the name of the Lord,
¹⁴ I will pay my vows to the Lord
   in the presence of all his people.

¹⁵ Precious in the sight of the Lord
   is the death of his saints.
¹⁶ O Lord, I am your servant;
   I am your servant, the son of your maidservant.
   You have loosed my bonds.

¹⁷ I will offer to you the sacrifice of thanksgiving
   and call on the name of the Lord.
¹⁸ I will pay my vows to the Lord
   in the presence of all his people,
¹⁹ in the courts of the house of the Lord,
   in your midst, O Jerusalem.
Praise the Lord!

OBSERVE	INTERPRET

KEY WORDS	DEFINITIONS	CROSS REFERENCES

MAIN POINT(S)

APPLY

PRAY

day *three*

READ

¹ Oh give thanks to the Lord, for he is good;
  for his steadfast love endures forever!

² Let Israel say,
  "His steadfast love endures forever."
³ Let the house of Aaron say,
  "His steadfast love endures forever."
⁴ Let those who fear the Lord say,
  "His steadfast love endures forever."

⁵ Out of my distress I called on the Lord;
  the Lord answered me and set me free.
⁶ The Lord is on my side; I will not fear.
  What can man do to me?
⁷ The Lord is on my side as my helper;
  I shall look in triumph on those who hate me.

⁸ It is better to take refuge in the Lord
  than to trust in man.
⁹ It is better to take refuge in the Lord
  than to trust in princes.

¹⁰ All nations surrounded me;
  in the name of the Lord I cut them off!
¹¹ They surrounded me, surrounded me on every side;
  in the name of the Lord I cut them off!
¹² They surrounded me like bees;
  they went out like a fire among thorns;
  in the name of the Lord I cut them off!
¹³ I was pushed hard, so that I was falling,
  but the Lord helped me.

¹⁴ The Lord is my strength and my song;
   he has become my salvation.
¹⁵ Glad songs of salvation
   are in the tents of the righteous:
"The right hand of the Lord does valiantly,
¹⁶   the right hand of the Lord exalts,
   the right hand of the Lord does valiantly!"
¹⁷ I shall not die, but I shall live,
   and recount the deeds of the Lord.
¹⁸ The Lord has disciplined me severely,
   but he has not given me over to death.

¹⁹ Open to me the gates of righteousness,
   that I may enter through them
   and give thanks to the Lord.
²⁰ This is the gate of the Lord;
   the righteous shall enter through it.
²¹ I thank you that you have answered me
   and have become my salvation.
²² The stone that the builders rejected
   has become the cornerstone.
²³ This is the Lord's doing;
   it is marvelous in our eyes.
²⁴ This is the day that the Lord has made;
   let us rejoice and be glad in it.

²⁵ Save us, we pray, O Lord!
   O Lord, we pray, give us success!

²⁶ Blessed is he who comes in the name of the Lord!
   We bless you from the house of the Lord.
²⁷ The Lord is God,
   and he has made his light to shine upon us.
Bind the festal sacrifice with cords,
   up to the horns of the altar!

²⁸ You are my God, and I will give thanks to you;
   you are my God; I will extol you.
²⁹ Oh give thanks to the Lord, for he is good;
   for his steadfast love endures forever!

OBSERVE	INTERPRET

KEY WORDS	DEFINITIONS	CROSS REFERENCES

MAIN POINT(S)

APPLY

PRAY

OUR HELP IS IN THE
NAME OF THE LORD, WHO
MADE HEAVEN AND EARTH.

PSALM 124:8

day *four*

PSALM 124

READ

[1] If it had not been the Lord who was on our side—
   let Israel now say—
[2] if it had not been the Lord who was on our side
   when people rose up against us,
[3] then they would have swallowed us up alive,
   when their anger was kindled against us;
[4] then the flood would have swept us away,
   the torrent would have gone over us;
[5] then over us would have gone
   the raging waters.

[6] Blessed be the Lord,
   who has not given us
   as prey to their teeth!
[7] We have escaped like a bird
   from the snare of the fowlers;
the snare is broken,
   and we have escaped!

[8] Our help is in the name of the Lord,
   who made heaven and earth.

OBSERVE	INTERPRET

KEY WORDS	DEFINITIONS	CROSS REFERENCES

MAIN POINT(S)	APPLY

PRAY

day *five*

1 Summarize what you learned from this week's thanksgiving psalms.	2 Which psalm or verse was your favorite? Explain.
3 Did you notice any common themes or elements in these psalms?	4 Provide an example of a psalmist's statement of desire to thank the Lord.
5 Often, thanksgiving psalms describe a crisis or time of distress. Share an example from one of this week's psalms.	6 Sometimes the psalmist shares a personal testimony of God's goodness. Can you find and jot down an example?

7 Was there a declaration of thanks that especially caught your attention?

8 Share a personal testimony of God's grace or mercy to you this week.

9 Thanksgiving psalms were often recited in concurrence with a thank offering. Record a specific thank offering you might present to God. This could be a gift of time, money, or other resources.

10 How can we develop a habit of giving thanks? Share and discuss with others.

11 What did you learn about God through these thanksgiving psalms?

12 What did you discover about how to worship God this week?

take it to *heart*

USE THIS SPACE TO WRITE OUT OR JOURNAL A FAVORITE VERSE FROM THIS WEEK'S STUDY, OR WRITE OUT YOUR OWN THANKSGIVING PSALM. (THIS IS BETWEEN YOU AND GOD.)

"BE STILL, AND KNOW
THAT I AM GOD. I WILL BE
EXALTED AMONG THE NATIONS,
I WILL BE EXALTED IN THE EARTH!"

PSALM 46:10

chapter *ten*

PRAISE PSALMS

take *note*

PRAISE PSALMS

take *note*

PRAISE PSALMS

day *one*

PSALM 8

READ

¹ O Lord, our Lord,
   how majestic is your name in all the earth!
You have set your glory above the heavens.
²   Out of the mouth of babies and infants,
you have established strength because of your foes,
   to still the enemy and the avenger.

³ When I look at your heavens, the work of your fingers,
   the moon and the stars, which you have set in place,
⁴ what is man that you are mindful of him,
   and the son of man that you care for him?

⁵ Yet you have made him a little lower than the heavenly beings
   and crowned him with glory and honor.
⁶ You have given him dominion over the works of your hands;
   you have put all things under his feet,
⁷ all sheep and oxen,
   and also the beasts of the field,
⁸ the birds of the heavens, and the fish of the sea,
   whatever passes along the paths of the seas.

⁹ O Lord, our Lord,
   how majestic is your name in all the earth!

OBSERVE

INTERPRET

KEY WORDS	DEFINITIONS	CROSS REFERENCES

MAIN POINT(S)	APPLY

PRAY

day *two*

PSALM 46

READ

¹ God is our refuge and strength,
   a very present help in trouble.
² Therefore we will not fear though the earth gives way,
   though the mountains be moved into the heart of the sea,
³ though its waters roar and foam,
   though the mountains tremble at its swelling.   *Selah*

⁴ There is a river whose streams make glad the city of God,
   the holy habitation of the Most High.
⁵ God is in the midst of her; she shall not be moved;
   God will help her when morning dawns.
⁶ The nations rage, the kingdoms totter;
   he utters his voice, the earth melts.
⁷ The Lord of hosts is with us;
   the God of Jacob is our fortress.   *Selah*

⁸ Come, behold the works of the Lord,
   how he has brought desolations on the earth.
⁹ He makes wars cease to the end of the earth;
   he breaks the bow and shatters the spear;
   he burns the chariots with fire.
¹⁰ "Be still, and know that I am God.
   I will be exalted among the nations,
   I will be exalted in the earth!"
¹¹ The Lord of hosts is with us;
   the God of Jacob is our fortress.   *Selah*

OBSERVE	INTERPRET

KEY WORDS	DEFINITIONS	CROSS REFERENCES

MAIN POINT(S)

APPLY

PRAY

day *three*

PSALM 95

READ

¹ Oh come, let us sing to the Lord;
   let us make a joyful noise to the rock of our salvation!
² Let us come into his presence with thanksgiving;
   let us make a joyful noise to him with songs of praise!
³ For the Lord is a great God,
   and a great King above all gods.
⁴ In his hand are the depths of the earth;
   the heights of the mountains are his also.
⁵ The sea is his, for he made it,
   and his hands formed the dry land.

⁶ Oh come, let us worship and bow down;
   let us kneel before the Lord, our Maker!
⁷ For he is our God,
   and we are the people of his pasture,
   and the sheep of his hand.
Today, if you hear his voice,
⁸   do not harden your hearts, as at Meribah,
   as on the day at Massah in the wilderness,
⁹ when your fathers put me to the test
   and put me to the proof, though they had seen my work.
¹⁰ For forty years I loathed that generation
   and said, "They are a people who go astray in their heart,
   and they have not known my ways."
¹¹ Therefore I swore in my wrath,
   "They shall not enter my rest."

OBSERVE	INTERPRET

KEY WORDS	DEFINITIONS	CROSS REFERENCES

MAIN POINT(S)

APPLY

PRAY

day *four*

PSALM 100

READ

1 Make a joyful noise to the Lord, all the earth!
2   Serve the Lord with gladness!
   Come into his presence with singing!

3 Know that the Lord, he is God!
   It is he who made us, and we are his;
   we are his people, and the sheep of his pasture.

4 Enter his gates with thanksgiving,
   and his courts with praise!
   Give thanks to him; bless his name!

5 For the Lord is good;
   his steadfast love endures forever,
   and his faithfulness to all generations.

OBSERVE	INTERPRET

KEY WORDS	DEFINITIONS	CROSS REFERENCES

MAIN POINT(S)	APPLY

PRAY

day *five*

PRAISE PSALMS | REVIEW & DISCUSSION QUESTIONS

1 Summarize what you learned from this week's praise psalms.	2 Which psalm or verse was your favorite? Explain.
3 Did you notice any common themes or elements in these psalms?	4 Provide an example of a psalmist's invitation to praise or a call to worship.
5 Often the psalmist provides a rationale or motive for praise. Share an example from one of this week's psalms.	6 The psalmist might conclude with a renewed call to praise God. Can you find an example?

7 How would you describe the difference between praise and thanksgiving?

8 Record a declaration of praise for God's greatness as Creator that especially caught your attention.

9 Share an example of the psalmist's praise for the mighty deeds of the Lord.

10 Could any of these psalms be sung to Jesus? Why or why not?

11 What did you learn about God through these praise psalms?

12 What did you discover about how to worship God this week?

take it to *heart*

USE THIS SPACE TO WRITE OUT OR JOURNAL A FAVORITE
VERSE FROM THIS WEEK'S STUDY, OR WRITE OUT YOUR
OWN PRAISE PSALM. (THIS IS BETWEEN YOU AND GOD.)

GREAT IS THE LORD, AND
GREATLY TO BE PRAISED,
AND HIS GREATNESS
IS UNSEARCHABLE.

PSALM 145:3

chapter *eleven*

PRAISE PSALMS

take *note*

PRAISE PSALMS

take *note*

PRAISE PSALMS

day *one*

PSALM 103

READ

¹ Bless the Lord, O my soul,
   and all that is within me,
   bless his holy name!
² Bless the Lord, O my soul,
   and forget not all his benefits,
³ who forgives all your iniquity,
   who heals all your diseases,
⁴ who redeems your life from the pit,
   who crowns you with steadfast love and mercy,
⁵ who satisfies you with good
   so that your youth is renewed like the eagle's.

⁶ The Lord works righteousness
   and justice for all who are oppressed.
⁷ He made known his ways to Moses,
   his acts to the people of Israel.
⁸ The Lord is merciful and gracious,
   slow to anger and abounding in steadfast love.
⁹ He will not always chide,
   nor will he keep his anger forever.
¹⁰ He does not deal with us according to our sins,
   nor repay us according to our iniquities.
¹¹ For as high as the heavens are above the earth,
   so great is his steadfast love toward those who fear him;
¹² as far as the east is from the west,
   so far does he remove our transgressions from us.
¹³ As a father shows compassion to his children,
   so the Lord shows compassion to those who fear him.
¹⁴ For he knows our frame;
   he remembers that we are dust.

¹⁵ As for man, his days are like grass;
   he flourishes like a flower of the field;
¹⁶ for the wind passes over it, and it is gone,
   and its place knows it no more.
¹⁷ But the steadfast love of the Lord is from everlasting to everlasting on those who fear him,
   and his righteousness to children's children,
¹⁸ to those who keep his covenant
   and remember to do his commandments.
¹⁹ The Lord has established his throne in the heavens,
   and his kingdom rules over all.

²⁰ Bless the Lord, O you his angels,
   you mighty ones who do his word,
   obeying the voice of his word!
²¹ Bless the Lord, all his hosts,
   his ministers, who do his will!
²² Bless the Lord, all his works,
   in all places of his dominion.
Bless the Lord, O my soul!

OBSERVE	INTERPRET

KEY WORDS	DEFINITIONS	CROSS REFERENCES

MAIN POINT(S)

APPLY

PRAY

day *two*

PSALM 145

---

[1] I will extol you, my God and King,
  and bless your name forever and ever.
[2] Every day I will bless you
  and praise your name forever and ever.
[3] Great is the Lord, and greatly to be praised,
  and his greatness is unsearchable.

[4] One generation shall commend your works to another,
  and shall declare your mighty acts.
[5] On the glorious splendor of your majesty,
  and on your wondrous works, I will meditate.
[6] They shall speak of the might of your awesome deeds,
  and I will declare your greatness.
[7] They shall pour forth the fame of your abundant goodness
  and shall sing aloud of your righteousness.

[8] The Lord is gracious and merciful,
  slow to anger and abounding in steadfast love.
[9] The Lord is good to all,
  and his mercy is over all that he has made.

[10] All your works shall give thanks to you, O Lord,
  and all your saints shall bless you!
[11] They shall speak of the glory of your kingdom
  and tell of your power,
[12] to make known to the children of man your mighty deeds,
  and the glorious splendor of your kingdom.
[13] Your kingdom is an everlasting kingdom,
  and your dominion endures throughout all generations.

[The Lord is faithful in all his words
   and kind in all his works.]
¹⁴ The Lord upholds all who are falling
   and raises up all who are bowed down.
¹⁵ The eyes of all look to you,
   and you give them their food in due season.
¹⁶ You open your hand;
   you satisfy the desire of every living thing.
¹⁷ The Lord is righteous in all his ways
   and kind in all his works.
¹⁸ The Lord is near to all who call on him,
   to all who call on him in truth.
¹⁹ He fulfills the desire of those who fear him;
   he also hears their cry and saves them.
²⁰ The Lord preserves all who love him,
   but all the wicked he will destroy.

²¹ My mouth will speak the praise of the Lord,
   and let all flesh bless his holy name forever and ever.

OBSERVE	INTERPRET

KEY WORDS	DEFINITIONS	CROSS REFERENCES

MAIN POINT(S)

APPLY

PRAY

I WILL PRAISE THE LORD
AS LONG AS I LIVE;
I WILL SING PRAISES TO MY GOD
WHILE I HAVE MY BEING.

PSALM 146:2

day *three*

PSALM 146

READ

¹ Praise the Lord!
Praise the Lord, O my soul!
² I will praise the Lord as long as I live;
   I will sing praises to my God while I have my being.

³ Put not your trust in princes,
   in a son of man, in whom there is no salvation.
⁴ When his breath departs, he returns to the earth;
   on that very day his plans perish.

⁵ Blessed is he whose help is the God of Jacob,
   whose hope is in the Lord his God,
⁶ who made heaven and earth,
   the sea, and all that is in them,
who keeps faith forever;
⁷   who executes justice for the oppressed,
   who gives food to the hungry.

The Lord sets the prisoners free;
⁸   the Lord opens the eyes of the blind.
The Lord lifts up those who are bowed down;
   the Lord loves the righteous.
⁹ The Lord watches over the sojourners;
   he upholds the widow and the fatherless,
   but the way of the wicked he brings to ruin.

¹⁰ The Lord will reign forever,
   your God, O Zion, to all generations.
Praise the Lord!

OBSERVE	INTERPRET

KEY WORDS	DEFINITIONS	CROSS REFERENCES

MAIN POINT(S)

APPLY

PRAY

day *four*

PSALM 148

READ

¹ Praise the Lord!
Praise the Lord from the heavens;
   praise him in the heights!
² Praise him, all his angels;
   praise him, all his hosts!

³ Praise him, sun and moon,
   praise him, all you shining stars!
⁴ Praise him, you highest heavens,
   and you waters above the heavens!

⁵ Let them praise the name of the Lord!
   For he commanded and they were created.
⁶ And he established them forever and ever;
   he gave a decree, and it shall not pass away.

⁷ Praise the Lord from the earth,
   you great sea creatures and all deeps,
⁸ fire and hail, snow and mist,
   stormy wind fulfilling his word!

⁹ Mountains and all hills,
   fruit trees and all cedars!
¹⁰ Beasts and all livestock,
   creeping things and flying birds!

¹¹ Kings of the earth and all peoples,
   princes and all rulers of the earth!
¹² Young men and maidens together,
   old men and children!

¹³ Let them praise the name of the Lord,
    for his name alone is exalted;
    his majesty is above earth and heaven.
¹⁴ He has raised up a horn for his people,
    praise for all his saints,
    for the people of Israel who are near to him.
Praise the Lord!

OBSERVE

INTERPRET

KEY WORDS	DEFINITIONS	CROSS REFERENCES

MAIN POINT(S)

APPLY

PRAY

day *five*

PRAISE PSALMS | REVIEW & DISCUSSION QUESTIONS

1 Summarize what you learned from this week's praise psalms.	2 Which psalm or verse was your favorite? Explain.
3 Did you notice any common themes or elements in these psalms?	4 Provide an example of a psalmist's invitation to praise or a call to worship.
5 Share a favorite call to worship from this week's psalms.	6 What motive or reason for praise stood out to you this week?

7 Of these praise songs, which renewed call to praise God motivated you to praise?

8 Record a declaration of praise for God's greatness as Creator that especially caught your attention.

9 Share an example from these psalms of praise that highlights the mighty deeds of the Lord.

10 Psalm 145 is an acrostic psalm utilizing the Hebrew alphabet. Try praising God using the letters of the alphabet.

11 What did you learn about God through these praise psalms?

12 What did you discover about how to worship God this week?

take it to *heart*

USE THIS SPACE TO WRITE OUT OR JOURNAL A FAVORITE VERSE FROM THIS WEEK'S STUDY, OR WRITE OUT YOUR OWN PRAISE PSALM. (THIS IS BETWEEN YOU AND GOD.)

LET THEM PRAISE
THE NAME OF THE LORD, FOR
HIS NAME ALONE IS EXALTED;
HIS MAJESTY IS ABOVE
EARTH AND HEAVEN.

PSALM 148:13

final *thoughts*

WRAPPING UP

final *thoughts*

End your study of Psalms this week by considering the following questions. Spend time reflecting on what God has revealed to you, through your inductive study of His Word, and how your heart and life have been changed by Him in the process.

1 Choose a favorite psalm or verse from this study. Explain why it's meaningful to you.	2 After completing this study, do you have a favorite category of psalm? Explain.
3 What overarching idea or theme from the psalms impacted you and why?	4 What did you learn about God through this study?

5 What did you learn about worship?

6 What did you learn about prayer?

7 Do the psalmists provide an example in some way that you'd like to follow?

8 In one sentence, how would you summarize and remember the Psalms?

9 Summarize this study in one word.

10 How are you transformed? How will you think or live differently because of this study?

pause and *reflect*

USE THIS SPACE TO WRITE OUT A PRAYER, A KEY PASSAGE, OR A REFLECTION ON YOUR STUDY OF PSALMS.

THE LORD WILL KEEP
YOUR GOING OUT
AND YOUR COMING IN
FROM THIS TIME FORTH
AND FOREVERMORE.

PSALM 121:8

leader *guide*

MAXIMIZING THE SMALL-GROUP EXPERIENCE

GO THEREFORE AND MAKE
DISCIPLES OF ALL NATIONS,
BAPTIZING THEM IN THE
NAME OF THE FATHER AND
OF THE SON AND OF THE
HOLY SPIRIT, TEACHING THEM
TO OBSERVE ALL THAT I
HAVE COMMANDED YOU.

MATTHEW 28:19-20

introduction

LEADING WOMEN THROUGH **SIMPLY BIBLE**

Welcome to SIMPLY BIBLE! Thank you for your commitment to walk alongside a group of women for this season of drawing near to God through His Word. In the midst of uncertainty, anxiety, and the cares of this world, what better place to lead women than to the honest prayers of the Psalms! Friend, we are in need of God's song in our hearts. Rather than allowing the emotions of life to become pent-up inside, these songs help us learn to seek His presence and work through pain and suffering.

Thank you for walking alongside others as they seek to honestly express their feelings with God. The primary objective of SIMPLY BIBLE is this:

> To inspire every woman to love God
> with all her heart, soul, mind and strength,
> and to love others as herself.
>
> LUKE 10:27

So breathe easy! Your role is simply to help facilitate that goal: to inspire women to love God and love others as herself. This does not entail becoming a walking commentary of Psalms or an expert in Hebrew poetry. Rather, the qualifications involve loving God and His Word with a desire to love and care for His women. That's it. Did you catch that? The prerequisite for leading this study is not Bible knowledge, it's love. Success depends on the heart.

SO GUARD YOUR HEART.

Ethos is a Latin word that denotes the fundamental character or spirit of a community, group, or person. When used to discuss dramatic literature, ethos is that moral element used to determine a character's action rather than his or her thought or emotion.[1] Ethos points to the inward being, to the moral fabric of the heart. In Biblical language, ethos absolutely compares to a person's heart. And our ethos, our heart, is important to God.

His Word tells us:

> Above all else, guard your heart,
> for everything you do flows from it.
>
> PROVERBS 4:23 (NIV)

Above all else, guard your heart. Why? Because everything we do flows from the heart, from our inward being. And that "everything" includes leading women through God's Word. If we want to see women growing in authentic relationships with Christ and with one another, that process must first begin in our own hearts.

> For the Lord sees not as man sees: man looks on the
> outward appearance, but the Lord looks on the heart.
>
> 1 SAMUEL 16:7

As individuals, ministry groups, and even churches, we often focus on outward appearances. I'm guilty. I call it "dressing up and playing church." When more time is spent designing beautiful handouts, creating engaging social media posts, coordinating impeccable table decorations and other "outward" items versus time spent on heart preparation, it might signal a problem. There is nothing wrong with making the outward beautiful. Yet, God looks at the heart. Is our primary focus there, too?

---

[1] **ethos.** Dictionary.com. *Dictionary.com Unabridged.* Random House, Inc. http://www.dictionary.com/browse/ethos (accessed: March 16, 2018).

When women hurt, the externals mean very little. Aside from a comforting cup of tea or coffee, it's love and hope overflowing from the heart that make a difference. To overflow with love and hope, hearts must be tapped into the power of His Spirit and His Word.

To effectively "guard our hearts" and prepare to lead women in inductive Bible study, three things are necessary:

(1) Jesus
(2) Prayer
(3) The Word

GUARDING YOUR HEART WITH **JESUS**

This may seem obvious, even "in your face" obvious. But honestly, isn't it easy for us to miss the forest for the trees? How can we expect others to believe if we ourselves are not believing? How will others trust if we do not trust? Apart from Jesus, we will not overflow with His Spirit and hope. Our efforts will ring hollow. Paul puts it this way:

> If I speak in the tongues of men and of angels, but have not love, I am a noisy gong or a clanging cymbal.
>
> 1 CORINTHIANS 13:1

None of us wants to be an annoying gong gone wrong. But without a personal heart connection to Christ's heart of love, we labor in our own strength. One friend refers to this kind of fruit as the "fake grapes" found in her Grandma's kitchen. Instead, we're seeking the juicy-sweet fruit of the Spirit that comes from abiding in the True Vine:

> Abide in me, and I in you. As the branch cannot bear fruit by itself, unless it abides in the vine, neither can you, unless you abide in me.
>
> JOHN 15:4

Abiding in Jesus is the secret, powerful ingredient to leading Bible study. Okay, maybe it's not so secret, but it is powerful! Some days, we feel that heart connection with God and other days we do not. Abiding is not a feeling. We know we abide as we seek to obey and follow His will. Fruit will follow.

An effective leader unifies her heart with Christ's humble and authentic heart. Are you daily abiding and aligning your character to Jesus from the inside out? Godly transformation happens as a woman applies Scripture, yields to God's will, and allows for the Spirit's holy work to happen within her own heart. That leads to true beauty. It's super attractive. Others will desire this kind of beauty and follow. Peter says it this way:

> Let your adorning be the hidden person of the heart
> with the imperishable beauty of a gentle and quiet spirit,
> which in God's sight is very precious.
>
> I PETER 3:4

GUARDING YOUR HEART WITH **PRAYER**

Here again, the need for prayer is obvious. Yet sometimes when caught up in preparation details, we overlook the obvious. Pray, pray, and pray! If Jesus required prayer in order to remain united with His Father, we surely require it more. Prayer keeps us focused on Christ and helps us remember that He is the Good Shepherd who ultimately leads our flocks to green pastures and quiet waters. As we study His Word, He will guide us in paths of righteousness. However, without Christ paving the way and clearing the path, we will struggle to get there. And so, we pray.

Set aside individual time to pray for Bible study. Before the semester begins, consider setting aside one day to commune with God. Be. Listen. Share. Sing. Seek. Surrender. Ponder. Commit. Once Bible study begins, allow for time to pray together as a group. Recognizing that prayer might be new for some, remind women to simply share their hearts and relate with God as the psalmists do. The acronym *P.R.A.Y.* provides an easy-to-follow template guiding groups through four steps of prayer:

P	PRAISE	Praise God for who He is.

Blessed be the God and Father of our Lord Jesus Christ!
I Peter 1:3

Short "popcorn prayers" of praise like Peter's easily allow everyone to participate. Simple words and phrases to worship God work best:

- I praise You, God, as the Light of the World.
- I praise You for You are Mighty to Save.
- Lord, You are Life.
- You are Truth.

Beginning group sessions with praise turns and focuses our hearts toward God.

R	REPENT	Confess and agree with God concerning sin.

If we confess our sins, he is faithful and just to forgive us our sins and to cleanse us from all unrighteousness.
I John 1:9

Offer group members a silent moment to allow for private confession.

A	ADORE	Admire and thank God for His ways.

Give thanks in all circumstances; for this is the will of God in Christ Jesus for you.
I Thessalonians 5:18

In the midst of trials, thanksgiving is a beautiful way to declare faith in God's goodness. Together, give thanks for all that God revealed during the study session.

Y	YIELD	Acknowledge your dependence on God. Yield to His ways.

Humble yourselves, therefore, under the mighty hand of God so that at the proper time he may exalt you, casting all your anxieties on him, because he cares for you.
I Peter 5:6-7

With Peter's encouragement, give every concern to the Lord!

With that, what sorts of things shall we yield to God? Here are a few ideas and ways to align with God's heart:

- May God be glorified through the study.
- May women begin to hunger and thirst for God and His Word.
- May God's will be accomplished in the hearts of women.
- May women believe in Jesus and cast their worries to Him.
- May women's hearts be united with His and with one another.
- May God offer protection from all distractions as women study His Word.
- May God's Word transform hearts and lives, that women would begin to think and live differently.

GUARDING YOUR HEART WITH **THE WORD**

Whether teaching a large group or facilitating a small group discussion, leaders are prone to fall into the trap of thinking that we need all the right answers. Furthermore, we think we need to be able to speak all those answers eloquently. Due to this false thinking, some leaders forget that love is the answer and spend countless hours scouring commentaries. They wear themselves out! God's Word is so deep and rich that the depths of a Scripture passage will not be plumbed in just one week. Thinking we need to have all the right answers is a fallacy.

Without a doubt, commentaries are valuable for checking one's interpretation. However, for leaders who spend too much time delving into commentaries versus pondering God's Word, the risk is that their workbooks and discussion will reflect the *commentaries* more than *Scripture itself*.

To counter this, we simply need time in God's Word. As we read, observe, and marinate in the Bible text itself, God's Spirit teaches and leads. His Word speaks on its own. It is powerful and effective. We can trust in it!

> So shall my word be that goes out from my mouth;
> it shall not return to me empty, but it shall
> accomplish that which I purpose, and shall
> succeed in the thing for which I sent it.
>
> ISAIAH 55:11

Read, read, and read again. As mentioned in the introduction, read the passage using various translations. Read aloud, and read slowly. Ponder. Listen to the Word while driving. Talk about what you are learning and discovering in the Word with family and friends. This will help you be prepared to speak when it is time for Bible study. Just as we marinate meat to soften, tenderize, and flavor it, we "sit in" the text, allowing God's Spirit to soften, tenderize, and flavor our hearts and minds with His personal message.

> I have stored up your word in my heart,
> that I might not sin against you.
>
> PSALM 119:11

A challenging, but brilliant way to soak in Scripture is memorization. Memorization is hard work, but the payoff is great. Scripture becomes embedded within our hearts and overflows when needed. Memorized scriptures guard my own heart. In leading, I have noticed that reciting or praying Scripture over women deeply touches their hearts, too. I highly encourage memorizing at least one key verse or passage from the study.

Ideally, teachers and small group leaders should prepare the study a week ahead of time. Yep! You read that right. Seek to be one week ahead of the regular study schedule in your personal study of the Word. If possible, allow time for leaders to review together before leading and teaching in groups the following week. The benefits of discussing, sharing, and grappling with the Word as leaders are priceless for preparation and confidence in facilitating discussion. Through it, God knits together the leaders' hearts. This will transform the *ethos* or heart of the group as a whole.

FRIENDS, MAY WE GUARD OUR HEARTS.

With Jesus, prayer, and His Word, we are well-equipped to love and lead transformative conversations around our Bible study tables.

> But you will receive power when the Holy Spirit
> has come upon you, and you will be my witnesses
> in Jerusalem and in all Judea and Samaria,
> and to the end of the earth.
>
> ACTS 1:8

The following tools and resources included in this appendix may provide additional help and support as you endeavor to lead your group. Use them however you find them to be helpful.

- Effective Leadership Guide
- Weekly Preparation Guide
- Bible Study Schedule
- Small Group Roster
- Attendance Record
- Prayer Log

effective *leadership*

A GUIDE TO LEADING A SMALL GROUP EFFECTIVELY

Remember that the goal for our study is to see women growing in relationship with Christ and one another. You do not need to be a Bible expert to lead women in discussion about His Word. You only need a heart to love and encourage women. So, what does effective small group leadership look like?

ENCOURAGING | In an encouraging small group, all participants feel included and welcome to share freely. Thoughts and ideas are respected, and women are cheered on in their efforts to grow closer to God through their study of His Word.

BIBLICALLY SOUND | When we endeavor to create a biblically-sound environment, we point women in the direction of truth and correct doctrine, gently guiding them away from wrong thinking.

BALANCED | In a group that is balanced, shy or quiet women are drawn out and encouraged to participate in discussions, while "over-sharers" are encouraged to listen to others and not to dominate the conversation.

WISE | A wise small group leader recognizes when the conversation is getting off-topic or veering toward gossip. In such situations, it is a good idea to redirect women back to the ultimate focus of the meeting: God's Word.

PRAYERFUL | A prayerful group leader is an asset to her group. She prays regularly for her group members and facilitates opportunities for them to pray for one another.

CONFIDENTIAL | Group members should feel secure that the things they share will remain confidential. An effective small group leader is committed to preserving the privacy of her group members.

weekly preparation guide

PREPARING FOR SMALL-GROUP MEETINGS

WEEK 1: WISDOM PSALMS

☐ Read the assigned daily passages.

☐ Use each daily framework to observe, interpret, and apply.

☐ Respond to all of the Day 5 questions.

☐ Pray for your small group meeting and for your group members.

1 What does this week's study tell me about God?	2 What does this week's study tell me about how I am to relate to Him?

WEEK 2: ROYAL PSALMS

☐ Read the assigned daily passages.

☐ Use each daily framework to observe, interpret, and apply.

☐ Respond to all of the Day 5 questions.

☐ Pray for your small group meeting and for your group members.

1 What does this week's study tell me about God?	2 What does this week's study tell me about how I am to relate to Him?

WEEK 3: LAMENT PSALMS

☐   Read the assigned daily passages.

☐   Use each daily framework to observe, interpret, and apply.

☐   Respond to all of the Day 5 questions.

☐   Pray for your small group meeting and for your group members.

1 What does this week's study tell me about God?	2 What does this week's study tell me about how I am to relate to Him?

WEEK 4: LAMENT PSALMS

☐   Read the assigned daily passages.

☐   Use each daily framework to observe, interpret, and apply.

☐   Respond to all of the Day 5 questions.

☐   Pray for your small group meeting and for your group members.

1 What does this week's study tell me about God?	2 What does this week's study tell me about how I am to relate to Him?

WEEK 5: COMMUNAL LAMENT PSALMS

☐ Read the assigned daily passages.

☐ Use each daily framework to observe, interpret, and apply.

☐ Respond to all of the Day 5 questions.

☐ Pray for your small group meeting and for your group members.

1 What does this week's study tell me about God?	2 What does this week's study tell me about how I am to relate to Him?

WEEK 6: PENITENTIAL PSALMS

☐ Read the assigned daily passages.

☐ Use each daily framework to observe, interpret, and apply.

☐ Respond to all of the Day 5 questions.

☐ Pray for your small group meeting and for your group members.

1 What does this week's study tell me about God?	2 What does this week's study tell me about how I am to relate to Him?

WEEK 7: TRUST PSALMS

- ☐ Read the assigned daily passages.

- ☐ Use each daily framework to observe, interpret, and apply.

- ☐ Respond to all of the Day 5 questions.

- ☐ Pray for your small group meeting and for your group members.

1 What does this week's study tell me about God?	2 What does this week's study tell me about how I am to relate to Him?

WEEK 8: PILGRIM PSALMS

- ☐ Read the assigned daily passages.

- ☐ Use each daily framework to observe, interpret, and apply.

- ☐ Respond to all of the Day 5 questions.

- ☐ Pray for your small group meeting and for your group members.

1 What does this week's study tell me about God?	2 What does this week's study tell me about how I am to relate to Him?

WEEK 9: THANKSGIVING PSALMS

☐ Read the assigned daily passages.

☐ Use each daily framework to observe, interpret, and apply.

☐ Respond to all of the Day 5 questions.

☐ Pray for your small group meeting and for your group members.

1 What does this week's study tell me about God?	2 What does this week's study tell me about how I am to relate to Him?

WEEK 10: PRAISE PSALMS

☐ Read the assigned daily passages.

☐ Use each daily framework to observe, interpret, and apply.

☐ Respond to all of the Day 5 questions.

☐ Pray for your small group meeting and for your group members.

1 What does this week's study tell me about God?	2 What does this week's study tell me about how I am to relate to Him?

WEEK 11: PRAISE PSALMS

☐ Read the assigned daily passages.

☐ Use each daily framework to observe, interpret, and apply.

☐ Respond to all of the Day 5 questions.

☐ Pray for your small group meeting and for your group members.

1 What does this week's study tell me about God?	2 What does this week's study tell me about how I am to relate to Him?

bible study *schedule*

PSALMS | A **SIMPLY BIBLE** STUDY

	READING ASSIGNMENT	SMALL GROUP MEETING DATE	LEADER MEETING DATE
WEEK 1			
WEEK 2			
WEEK 3			
WEEK 4			
WEEK 5			
WEEK 6			
WEEK 7			
WEEK 8			
WEEK 9			
WEEK 10			
WEEK 11			

small group *roster*

PSALMS | A **SIMPLY BIBLE** STUDY

PARTICIPANT LIST

1

2

3

4

5

6

7

8

9

10

11

12

13

14

15

NAME

BIRTHDAY
PHONE NUMBER
EMAIL ADDRESS
CONTACT METHOD

NOTES

NAME

BIRTHDAY
PHONE NUMBER
EMAIL ADDRESS
CONTACT METHOD

NOTES

NAME

BIRTHDAY
PHONE NUMBER
EMAIL ADDRESS
CONTACT METHOD

NOTES

NAME

BIRTHDAY

PHONE NUMBER

EMAIL ADDRESS

CONTACT METHOD

NOTES

NAME

BIRTHDAY

PHONE NUMBER

EMAIL ADDRESS

CONTACT METHOD

NOTES

NAME

BIRTHDAY

PHONE NUMBER

EMAIL ADDRESS

CONTACT METHOD

NOTES

NAME

BIRTHDAY	
PHONE NUMBER	
EMAIL ADDRESS	
CONTACT METHOD	

NOTES

NAME

BIRTHDAY	
PHONE NUMBER	
EMAIL ADDRESS	
CONTACT METHOD	

NOTES

NAME

BIRTHDAY	
PHONE NUMBER	
EMAIL ADDRESS	
CONTACT METHOD	

NOTES

NAME

BIRTHDAY	
PHONE NUMBER	
EMAIL ADDRESS	
CONTACT METHOD	

NOTES

NAME

BIRTHDAY	
PHONE NUMBER	
EMAIL ADDRESS	
CONTACT METHOD	

NOTES

NAME

BIRTHDAY	
PHONE NUMBER	
EMAIL ADDRESS	
CONTACT METHOD	

NOTES

NAME

BIRTHDAY	
PHONE NUMBER	
EMAIL ADDRESS	
CONTACT METHOD	

NOTES

NAME

BIRTHDAY	
PHONE NUMBER	
EMAIL ADDRESS	
CONTACT METHOD	

NOTES

NAME

BIRTHDAY	
PHONE NUMBER	
EMAIL ADDRESS	
CONTACT METHOD	

NOTES

attendance log

PSALMS | A **SIMPLY BIBLE** STUDY

PARTICIPANT'S NAME	WEEK 1	WEEK 2	WEEK 3	WEEK 4	WEEK 5	WEEK 6	WEEK 7	WEEK 8	WEEK 9	WEEK 10	WEEK 11
1											
2											
3											
4											
5											
6											
7											
8											
9											
10											
11											
12											
13											
14											
15											

I AM THE VINE; YOU
ARE THE BRANCHES.
WHOEVER ABIDES IN ME
AND I IN HIM, HE IT IS
THAT BEARS MUCH FRUIT,
FOR APART FROM ME
YOU CAN DO NOTHING.

JOHN 15:5

prayer log

PSALMS | A **SIMPLY BIBLE** STUDY

DATE	NAME	REQUEST	FOLLOW-UP

prayer log

PSALMS | A **SIMPLY BIBLE** STUDY

DATE	NAME	REQUEST	FOLLOW-UP

prayer log

DATE	NAME	REQUEST	FOLLOW-UP

prayer log

DATE	NAME	REQUEST	FOLLOW-UP

prayer log

PSALMS | A **SIMPLY BIBLE** STUDY

DATE	NAME	REQUEST	FOLLOW-UP

AND WE KNOW THAT
FOR THOSE WHO LOVE GOD
ALL THINGS WORK TOGETHER
FOR GOOD, FOR THOSE WHO
ARE CALLED ACCORDING
TO HIS PURPOSE.

ROMANS 8:28

Made in the USA
Las Vegas, NV
04 January 2024

83900463R00190